THE ABOLITION
OF THE SLAVE TRADE
IN ENGLAND,
1784–1807

THE ABOLITION OF THE SLAVE TRADE IN ENGLAND,

1784-1807

by

Dale H. Porter

ARCHON BOOKS
1970

© Copyright 1970 by Dale H. Porter
ALL RIGHTS RESERVED

ISBN: 0 208 00896 9
Library of Congress Catalog Card Number: 71-107956

HT
1162
.P65

PRINTED IN THE UNITED STATES OF AMERICA

To Betty Joe

CONTENTS

Abbreviations	viii
Preface	ix
Introduction	1
The Defenders of the Slave Trade	16
Prelude to Abolition	30
The Case Against Abolition	52
The Parliamentary Conflict, 1789–1792	70
The Parliamentary Conflict, 1793–1803	89
War and Trade in the West Indies, 1792–1804	108
The Politics of Abolition	125
Conclusion	140
Appendix I: Average Prices of Sugar, 1793–1806	144
Appendix II: Sugar Retained for Consumption in Great Britain, 1791–1806	145
Bibliography	146
Index	159

ABBREVIATIONS IN THE FOOTNOTES

British Museum Additional Manuscripts .... BM Add MS
House of Commons Sessional Papers .... HC Sess Pap
Public Record Office Manuscripts:
    Board of Trade, or Privy Council
    Committee for Trade & Plantations .... BT
    Colonial Office Papers .... CO
    Foreign Office Papers .... FO
    Privy Council Office Records .... PC
    Public Record Office Special Collections ... PRO

The report of the Privy Council Committee for Trade and Plantations published in 1789 has never been paginated. It is nearly 800 pages long and loosely organized. Hence precise citations are not possible. It is abbreviated throughout in footnotes as: PC Rpt 1789.
Works cited in the footnotes after their first appearance have been cited by author and short title except for Robert I. and Samuel Wilberforce, *The Life of William Wilberforce* (5 vols., London, 1838) which is cited throughout as *Life of Wilberforce*.

Preface

Most students of history dismiss the abolition of the British slave trade with "Oh, Wilberforce and all that." The identification of abolition with this one evangelical reformer is not due to a lack of information on the subject. It is, rather, part of a long tradition established by the abolitionists themselves and carried on by generations of otherwise critical historians. The first full-length account of abolition was published in 1808 by Thomas Clarkson, a leading figure in the movement, who saw in the victory of his ideals a manifestation of divine favor. The five-volume biography of William Wilberforce published by his sons in 1838, packed with the reformer's own letters and diary entries, echoed Clarkson's theme. These two works, added to the parliamentary debates and the vast amount of propaganda published during the campaign for abolition, have furnished most of the material from which histories of the antislavery movement have been drawn. Wilberforce's opponents, on the other hand, were neither prolific nor popular writers; and so their views and their alleged motives have come down to us principally through the unsympathetic media mentioned above.

It is difficult to use the records left by "Wilberforce and Co."

without absorbing some of their moralistic attitudes. As long as one is writing about the anti-slavery movement, this difficulty may be harmless. But most accounts of the abolitionists include observations on the parliamentary legislation involved and on the causes of its success or failure. Here the traditional story fails to satisfy objective criteria. For by concentrating on certain individuals and their style of agitation historians have blinded themselves to political, economic, and individual human factors of equal or greater importance to the success of abolition. Wilberforce himself warned against this tendency in a letter in 1792*:

> In point of fact great political events are rarely the offspring of cool, deliberate system; they receive their shape, size, and colour, and the data of their existence, from a thousand causes which could hardly have been foreseen, and in the production of which, various unconnected and jarring parties have combined and assisted.

This statement describes almost perfectly what happened in the history of abolition. No single group of advocates and no cohesive set of events determined the decisions of Parliament. The motives of the 283 members who voted for the final legislation will never be fully revealed. But by concentrating on the activities and arguments of the defenders of the British slave trade, and by examining in manuscript collections the not-so-public background to the parliamentary campaign, it is possible to reconstruct some of the unforeseen developments and personal relationships which played such a large part in the story.

Anyone seeking to revise the traditional approach to British abolition cannot ignore Eric Williams' arresting *Capitalism and Slavery* (1944). The idea that slavery provided the foundation for British industrial development, only to be destroyed by matured capitalist interests, is certainly useful. In developing

*Robert and Samuel Wilberforce, *The Life of William Wilberforce* (5 vols., London, 1838), II, 7.

PREFACE   xi

his general theme, however, Williams lumped abolition and
emancipation together and neglected too many circumstances
peculiar to the former movement. J. D. Fage, in his introduction to the 1964 edition of Sir Reginald Coupland's *The British Anti-Slavery Movement*, admirably delineates the contributions and limitations of both Coupland and Williams.

To most readers it will be plain that I have not been sympathetic to William Wilberforce's evangelical style of argument. While recognizing his eloquence and determination, I grew annoyed by his over-riding insistence, session after parliamentary session, on his own solution to the problem of the slave trade. It is hard for me to measure the effect of these feelings. I have tried to understand why the majority of members of Parliament refused to sanction the abolitionists' proposals for sixteen consecutive years, and then finally reversed their position. If in my account Wilberforce and his friends appear hasty, narrow-minded, or even ignorant, it is because the members of Parliament and the public often saw them that way, and said so.

No attempt has been made to whitewash the defenders of the slave trade. The task would be futile at best. It became clear in the last years of the abolition campaign that the West Indian planters were as much socially as economically tied to the institution of slavery, that the process of defining and defending their position had deepened their conservatism, and that no plan short of parliamentary legislation would induce them to alter the traditional organization of the plantation economy. On the other hand, when abolition was first proposed the arguments of its opponents were timely and effective. In showing why this was so, I have necessarily presented the case in terms more favorable than its past or present enemies would consider just.

This book, and the study leading to it, were made possible by a fellowship from the Danforth Foundation of St. Louis, for which I am most grateful. Special thanks are due to Professors Robert W. Smith and Robert Lang of the University of Oregon, and Ian R. Christie of the University of London, for their helpful criticism and guidance; to the staffs of the Institute of Historical Research, the British Museum, and the Public Record Office, London, for their generous cooperation; and to the West India Committee of London and the Merchant Venturers' Society of Bristol, for permission to use their archives.

1

Introduction

The abolition of the British slave trade was formally proposed in 1788 and finally enacted by Parliament in 1807. The arguments for and against legislation which filled the intervening years, were replete with prejudice, hearsay, misrepresentation, and bitter invective. What follows is not another general introduction to the subject,[1] but an attempt to formulate some reasonably objective statements about the slave trade and the West Indian economy.

British merchant shippers had been transporting Negro slaves from Africa to the West Indies since the end of the 16th century. What began as a modest venture, operated by a chartered company, gradually became an extensive and highly competitive trade. By 1775, when the British West Indies had reached the peak of their prosperity, and when non-British territories were rapidly expanding, merchants from London, Liverpool, and Bristol carried nearly 60,000 slaves a year across the Atlantic.

[1]The best short introduction is Eveline C. Martin, "The English Slave Trade and the African Settlements," in *The Cambridge History of the British Empire* (Cambridge, 1929), I. A longer, more popular account is Daniel P. Mannix, *Black Cargoes; a History of the African Slave Trade, 1518–1865* (New York, 1962).

During the American Revolution the slave trade was discouraged by French and colonial American privateers. Peacetime recovery was slow. By 1787 British traders still had not regained their former level of human exports.[2] In that year some 137 ships with a combined tonnage of 22,263 and with crews of about 5,000 men sailed from British ports to trade for slaves on the African coast. They carried British goods worth £401,593 and foreign exports (including East India cottons) worth another £266,661. Part of the goods were delivered to the British factories on the coast, part to private black dealers for slaves. Paying goods worth about £15 for adult male slaves in good health, less for females and children, the merchants collected 38,000 to 42,000 Negroes. With them the ships began the difficult eight-week journey across the Atlantic. Because of the frightful conditions on board, perhaps only 34,000 remained alive when they reached the West Indies. There they were sold for an average £35 each to English, French, Dutch, Danish, and Spanish proprietors, either directly or through agents.[3]

This is a fair description as far as it goes, but it suggests a rigid pattern of trade where none existed. "A simple exchange of cargo for Negroes, on the African coast, their sale in the West Indies, and the remittance of the proceeds, cannot be regarded as usual, characteristic, or even representative."[4] Slaving in the late 18th century was actually a variable and complex business involving the services of bankers, manufacturers, shipowners, plantation owners, and a host of minor agents and tradesmen. Some of these services need to be explained because they are important to the history of abolition.

The organization of the British slave trade centered in Liver-

[2] Cf. *HC Sess Pap* 1789(573–576)LXXI.
[3] Franz Hochstetter, "Die Wirtschaftlichen und Politischen Motive für die Abschaffung des Britischen Sklavenhandels im Jahre 1806/1807," in Gustav Schmoller, ed., *Staats- und Socialwissenschaftliche Forschungen* (Leipzig, 1878–1908), XXV, part I, 12–13. There are few reliable statistics on 18th-century trade, but Hochstetter's figures are approximately correct.
[4] F. E. Hyde, B. B. Parkinson, and S. Marriner, "The Nature and Profitability of the Liverpool Slave Trade," *Economic History Review*, Series 2, V(1953), 372.

INTRODUCTION 3

pool and Bristol. Aggressiveness, specialization, and proximity to the manufacturers of African trade goods had helped the former town overcome the lead of the latter in the first half of the century. In 1787 Liverpool sent 78 ships totalling 13,700 tons to Africa, whereas Bristol sent only 31 ships totalling 4,236 tons.[5] A few ships also cleared from London, Lancaster, and Poole. None came from Scotland.[6]

Within Liverpool the trade was yet further concentrated. According to a deposition laid before Parliament by one of the town's delegates, in March 1790 a total of 139 Liverpool ships was employed in slaving, of which half were owned by only eight companies. The other half were scattered among another thirty-one owners.[7] Liverpool slave merchants often engaged in other kinds of shipping, as well as banking and insurance. Some of them traded to North America and Europe. Few, if any, depended solely on slaves for a livelihood.[8]

Around Liverpool a network of small manufacturers and tradesmen supplied the "trade goods" used for barter in Africa —beads, textiles, ironmongery, brass bars, cheap rifles, liquor, and so on—and generally fitted out the ships for each new venture.[9] The gun trade of Birmingham, for example, was said to involve between 4,000 and 5,000 persons, who in peacetime depended largely on orders for Africa. Suppliers of trade goods around Manchester employed "upwards of 18,000" men, women and children.[10] In Liverpool itself, participation in the trade was almost a community affair, as a local writer explained in 1795:

[5]*HC Sess Pap* 1789(631)LXXXII, 5–7. By 1798 the ratio between Liverpool and Bristol was 160 to 3, with 8 ships from London. Lowell J. Ragatz, *The Fall of the Planter Class in the British Caribbean, 1763–1833* (New York, 1928), 83.
[6]*HC Sess Pap* 1789(629)LXXXII.
[7]*HC Sess Pap* 1790(698)LXXXVII, 500–509.
[8]Hyde et. al., "Nature and Profitability of the Slave Trade," 373–374.
[9]Lists of goods and trades concerned are found in Ragatz, *Fall of the Planter Class*, 84; in Gomer Williams, *History of the Liverpool Privateers and Letters of Marque*. (London, 1897), 545–547; and in *HC Sess Pap* 1789(573–576)LXXXI.
[10]*PC Rpt 1789*, part IV, #3, items 2 and 4.

Almost every order of people is interested in a Guinea cargo ... he who cannot send a bale, will send a bandbox.... It is well known that many of the small vessels that import about an hundred slaves are fitted out by attorneys, drapers, ropers, grocers, tallow-chandlers, barbers, tailors, etc.; some have one-eighth [share in a ship's capital], some a fifteenth, some a thirty-second.[11]

In view of the hazards of such a long voyage, with a human cargo liable to disease and death, and with an uncertain market at the end, it is surprising that the slave trade should have attracted such interest. Ships were often lost at sea and longterm profits were not especially high. Yet it was a highly speculative trade. A major success could make a man's fortune or compensate for a run of bad luck.[12]

Not all the cargo from Liverpool and Bristol was exchanged for Negroes on the African coast. Wood and ivory were common purchases, especially if Negroes were scarce and the slaving captain in a hurry. Most English ships also bought enough fresh provisions along the coast to last through the Atlantic passage. Together with cheap cloth, gold and curios, these goods made up a fair-sized "legitimate" trade which abolitionists were to hold up as an alternative to slaving.

A striking proportion of the 38,000 to 42,000 slaves purchased annually by the British traders in Africa were destined for nonBritish territories on the other side of the ocean. George Hibbert, a London slave and sugar merchant, estimated that 15,567 slaves were annually imported, and remained, in the

[11]Anonymous, *A General and Descriptive History of Liverpool*, quoted in Ramsay Muir, *A History of Liverpool* (London, 1907), 194–195.
[12]Hochstetter, "Motive für die Abschaffung," 63, put the profit at 9% as opposed to 12% in the American trade. Lord Hawkesbury, in his cautious preface to the *PC Rpt 1789*, wrote "It is a matter of much doubt whether the excess of the gains after deducting the losses incurred in the trade have exceeded the advantages to be derived from other commerce." See also BM Add MS 38416, 130–131, James Jones (Liverpool merchant and Jamaican legislator) to Hawkesbury, ca. June 1788.

INTRODUCTION

British West Indies,[13] leaving 23,000 to 27,000 for other Caribbean buyers. The foreign market for slaves had been built up during the 18th century with the approval of the British government. According to the economic ideas of the day, slaves were a commodity whose sale abroad would help the balance of trade. Not until later did slaves come to be seen as factors of production and hence responsible for the upsurge of foreign competition in the sugar market.

Before 1775 the British slave merchants faced little competition in foreign markets. Their proximity to supplies of cheap trade goods, and their superior financial organization, gave them a great advantage over other European traders. But the period between the American and French Revolutions saw determined efforts by France, Spain, and the United States to free themselves from dependence on Liverpool. Aggressive merchants from Massachusetts, Rhode Island, and South Carolina were reported to have vastly expanded their trade to Africa immediately after the revolutionary war, and by 1790 they were even fitting out in English ports to save money.[14] Most of them were supplying the southern States, but they found it easy to ship by way of the Caribbean to pick up extra business.

Spain, having gained two small islands off the Cameroons coast in 1778, tried hard to establish her own slave trade.[15] At the outbreak of war with England in 1779, her trade was thrown open to all Spanish subjects in Spanish or neutral vessels, a move designed to throw off her dependence on the English. In 1783 the Spanish Crown proscribed all foreign vessels. But despite strong encouragement from official agencies, no Spanish merchant was able to carry on alone. Finally a contract for

[13] *HC Sess Pap* 1790(698)LXXXVII, 392. Most slave traders questioned by Parliamentary committees in 1789–91 stated that two-thirds of the British slave trade went to foreign areas.
[14] *HC Sess Pap* 1790(698)LXXXVII, 191, testimony of James Baillie, London merchant.
[15] The Spanish colonies, after the demise of the Asiento contract in 1750, were supplied by the British via Jamaica and Cuba. Thomas Baines, *History of the Commerce and Town of Liverpool* (London, 1852), 477.

4,000 slaves was given to Edward Barry, an Englishman, and another to the firm of Baker and Dawson of Liverpool.[16] This was a make-shift arrangement, however, and the Spanish government left no doubt of the intention to get rid of it as soon as Spanish subjects were prepared to trade for themselves.

What the Spanish were attempting the French had already accomplished to a degree which threatened ruin to a major part of the British slave trade. Before 1778 the French had imported 14,000 to 15,000 Africans a year in their own ships, while purchasing even more from the British. For reasons similar to those of Spain, the French government proclaimed in 1784 a bounty of 40 livres per ton for every ship bound for Africa from a French port. For every slave imported into the French West Indies on a French ship there was another bounty of 60 to 100 livres. In addition, all the French islands except those in the Windward group imposed a toll of 6 livres each on slaves imported by the British.[17]

It is true that in the beginning the new traders depended on British captains and British supplies and that a great many "French" slaves were in fact bought from English factors on the African coast.[18] But what little revenue England gained in this manner was more than offset by French advances in commerce and navigation. After acquiring, by the peace treaty of 1783, two trading stations on the African coast and a share of the lucrative business at Bonny and Old Calabar, the French built a fleet of slaving vessels twice the size of those used by the British.[19] In the judgment of John Yates, a slave trader of almost twenty years' experience:

[16]William Eden to Hawkesbury, BM Add MS 38416, 114–116. James Jones reported (*Ibid.*, 216) that "Dawson's contract was for 3,000 slaves certain and he may import as many as 7,000." Another company [illegible but probably Tarleton of Tarleton and Backhouse, Liverpool] "have a similar contract with the Spanish for an equal number...."
[17]Hochstetter, "Motive für die Abschaffung," 66–67, and *PC Rpt 1789*, part I, "Special Information."
[18]Baines, *History of Liverpool*, 477; BM Add MS 38416, 9, 89; *PC Rpt 1789*, part IV, testimony of Baillie, King, and Herbert.
[19]*HC Sess Pap* 1790(698)LXXXVII, 478 ff., testimony of several British admirals.

INTRODUCTION 7

It is now nothing but a little Superior knowledge of the Trade, (that of purchasing Slaves upon some parts of the Coast) that the English support themselves by. And in a little time no doubt but the French will become equal masters of it, from their legislative encouragement.[20]

Unfortunately the only figures which might test Yates' report were supplied by other slave merchants, while opposing the Slave Trade Regulating Bill of 1788. The figures are repeated here because there is no evidence or motive for distortion in this particular part of the testimony. The figures appear conservative beside most other estimates, and they were used by both abolitionists and their opponents for at least ten years. The number of slaves annually exported from Africa was given as follows: 38,000 by the British, 20,000 by the French, 10,000 by the Portuguese, 4,000 by the Dutch, and 2,000 by the Danes.[21] Henry Brougham, in a later, careful criticism, corrected the figure for French imports to 30,000, and Hochstetter arrived at the same conclusion.[22] If they were correct, it shows that the French had doubled their share of the trade in ten years, and were indeed threatening the British position.

To circumvent the restrictions imposed by foreign colonial powers, the British established free ports in several West Indian islands from which slaves could be re-exported in foreign ships without tariff charges. An average of 9,488 slaves per year was sold through the free ports between 1788 and 1792;[23] and with them, to the delight of the mother country, went a large volume of British manufactures.

In the non-British West Indies slaves were retailed by independent agents or sold directly to planters. Payment was made in cash and sometimes in produce. While this had formerly been

[20]PRO 30/8:193, Yates to Pitt, July 1788.
[21]*PC Rpt 1789*, part IV, #14.
[22]Henry Brougham, *An Inquiry into the Colonial Policy of the European Powers* (4 vols., Edinburgh, 1803), I, 531. Hochstetter, "Motive für die Abschaffung," 66.
[23]Frances Armytage, *The Free Port System in the British West Indies* (London, 1953), 65.

the case in the British islands, after about 1760 financial difficulties made it increasingly rare. The planters, having fallen into debt to their factors in England, began to export their produce on consignment, in the factors' ships, in order to pay off the loans.[24]

The slave merchants were often short of capital, the income from one voyage being used to finance the next. They could not afford to extend the planters long-term credit. But the planters had no ready money with which to buy slaves. Therefore both turned again to a West India factor, usually one of the merchant-bankers of London with extensive connections in the colonies. The factor's agent purchased the slaves with short-term bills of exchange, payable soon after the slave ship arrived in England. Then the agent resold the slaves to the planters on long-term credit, using for security the produce shipped to the agent's firm in England.[25]

Thus the Liverpool merchants were protected from financial entanglements in the West Indies. But they were also isolated from the political influence which the West India planters wielded in London. This isolation was to prove dangerous during the campaign against the slave trade, whenever the interests of Liverpool differed from those of the planters and their factors.

The changes in the financing of the British slave trade during the latter half of the 18th century were occasioned, to repeat, by the West Indian planters' growing indebtedness. What had once been the most prosperous part of the British Empire was now in a state of economic decline. The appearance of new rivals, the loss of valuable markets, financial imprudence, and the constant need to purchase new slaves had all played a part in that development; and each element was important to the history of abolition.

The British West Indies formed one part of a network of

[24]Richard Pares, *Merchants and Planters* (Cambridge, 1960), 47. The planters had to sell produce in England to obtain sterling, because the factors would not accept colonial paper money in payment of debts.
[25]R. B. Sheridan, "The Commercial and Financial Organization of the British Slave Trade, 1750-1807," *Economic History Review*, Series 2, XI, 260.

INTRODUCTION 9

trade that existed between Britain and her trans-Atlantic possessions. The Caribbean planters held a monopoly of the British sugar market, exchanging their yearly crops for manufactures and household supplies in the mother country. They also bartered rum and molasses, the by-products of sugar, for lumber and food supplies from the North American colonies. Until about 1763, this double arrangement guaranteed the planters cheap supplies and high prices. But at the end of the Seven Years' War, several productive Caribbean islands were ceded to England by France, islands whose produce was immediately thrown onto the protected British market. The older British West Indies had suffered severely during the War and their recovery was impeded by the new competition.

When the American colonies rebelled in 1776, the cost of lumber and provisions nearly doubled. Some of the West Indies were struck by famine as a result of the interruption of trade. The market for rum and molasses also diminished. Peace brought further disappointment, for in 1783 the British government issued an Order-in-Council placing the new American states outside the old navigation laws. The old pattern of trade, so essential to West Indian profits, was destroyed. By 1789 the average Jamaica planter was making no more than 4% on his investment, or just enough to cover depreciation,[26] and no relief was in sight.

The American crisis might not have been so crippling had the West Indian economy been basically strong. But in the golden years before 1775, planters had amended the rule of inheritance by primogeniture by charging their estates with annuities for younger sons, wives, mothers, and friends, and with marriage portions for daughters.[27] The amounts involved were large even for a period of prosperity; when profits fell they became a disastrous burden.[28]

Absenteeism was another cause of economic weakening in the

[26]*PC Rpt 1789*, part III, A, #53. Depreciation estimate in *HC Sess Pap* 1807(65)III, appendix, II.
[27]Pares, *Merchants and Planters*, 42.
[28]*HC Sess Pap* 1807(65)III, 39, testimony of Charles Bosanquet. A detailed example is in R. Pares, *A West India Fortune* (New Haven, Archon reprint, 1968), 142.

West Indies. Too often the planters left their estates in the hands of subordinates and returned to England to live off the revenues. The local attorneys usually appointed as overseers for the estates were not noted for close supervision, and the managers they hired were often unscrupulous. In any event their sole concern was to maintain production levels, regardless of long-term waste in men, money, and machines. The absentee planter, even if he wished it, had little real control over these men, and he was left "the choice between eternal friction on the one hand and a gentle decline into bankruptcy on the other."[29]

Whatever the financial acumen of the British planter, he could not avoid one constant expense: the purchase of new slaves. A primary fact about the slave population in the West Indies was its tendency to diminish without regular imports from Africa. The number of slaves reaching working age was, as a general rule in all the islands, 3% to 5% less than the annual number of deaths. Decline had been the rule throughout the 18th century, and though there were exceptional estates from time to time, no island, not even one long settled like Barbados,[30] had ever managed to make up the overall deficiency.

Many reasons were offered for this state of affairs. Many of them were of doubtful validity, but one was obvious to everyone:

> ... there was an unhappy lack of proportion between the sexes; less than one third of the slaves imported were women. In 1789, there was an excess of 30,000 males in Jamaica alone. Then too, but slight attempt was made to establish a balance on a given property, the ratio at times being as great as five men to one female.[31]

[29]Pares, *A West India Fortune*, 142. For a complete discussion of the problem see L. J. Ragatz, *Absentee Landlordism in the British West Indies* (London, 1929), *passim*.
[30]David Makinson, *Barbados: A Study of North American-West Indian Relations, 1739–1789* (The Hague, 1964), 15, table I, shows that the Negro population of that island declined over 25% between 1773 and 1786.
[31]Ragatz, *Fall of the Planter Class*, 34.

INTRODUCTION   11

In these circumstances the Negro population had little chance of increasing its size by natural means.

Three other causes of population decline were disease, weather, and "seasoning." Slaves, especially the young, were more susceptible than whites to measles, smallpox, cholera, and such diseases, and epidemics passed through the islands from time to time, killing off thousands. Drought was frequent in the older islands and hurricanes occurred almost everywhere. From 1783 to 1786 the West Indies were subjected to a spate of diseases and damaging winds that ruined crops and reduced the slave population considerably.[32]

"Seasoning", unlike the other two dangers, affected everyone. That is, every new arrival from Africa underwent a period of about three years of easy training, during which time his body adjusted to the West Indian climate, food, and disease—or he died. To a lesser extent the same ordeal awaited white immigrants, although they usually had the advantages of leisure and constant medical attention. But during the campaign to end the slave trade, while abolitionists pointed with horror to Negro deaths, anti-abolitionists used the fact of white susceptibility as proof of the necessity of employing Negro labor.

Little can be said with certainty about food and the severity of labor as causes of population decline. Claims and counterclaims flew back and forth in great volume during the 1790's, but all seem to have been based on isolated records or reports, often distorted, from which no generally valid statement could be made. Sickness and weather attacks, however, were selective in their destruction, and many estates escaped harm for long periods of time; yet almost none were capable of increasing their labor forces by natural means. Again, "seasoning" inflated the West Indian rate of mortality but it could hardly have caused that which necessitated new imports. The only remaining suspects are social chaos, food, and excessive labor. And for all three the planters were finally responsible.

Two principal explanations exist for the planters' tendency

[32]Cf. H. C. Bell, "British Commercial Policy in the West Indies, 1783-93" in the *English Historical Review*, XXXI (1916), 431-432.

to ignore "conditions making impossible the healthy growth of a domesticated creole stock."[33] The more charitable, circulated by Wilberforce whenever he wished to placate the opposition, was that the planters were indeed anxious to improve conditions for their slaves, but were too often absent from their estates to ensure progress. The other explanation is based on planters' price estimates. The cost of raising a creole slave from birth to age 18, when he might be used in productive field work, was about £5 sterling per year, or £90 altogether.[34] A healthy new adult African, on the other hand, could be secured and seasoned for £50 to £70. The advantage of importing over breeding was obvious. That new slaves were readily available on long-term credit merely reinforced the planters' tendency to bypass the trouble of raising their own.

Less noticeable to residents in the West Indies, but no less costly in the long run, was the proliferation of household servants and miscellaneous laborers contributing little or nothing to the estate's net revenue. They had been deemed necessary or convenient at some past moment and were now not to be removed, least of all to the hard-working field gang. The proportion of these menials was often astonishing, even to contemporaries in England. To the redundant might be added those too young, too old, or too sick to work. On one Jamaica estate at the beginning of 1792, no less than 40% of the slaves were unfit for field work.[35]

The proliferation of auxiliary slaves, together with soil exhaustion,[36] population decline, and the gradual expansion of existing plantations, occasioned a moderate but steady importation of slaves into the settled parts of the British sugar islands. A far different demand came from territories just being opened

[33] Ragatz, *Fall of the Planter Class*, 36.
[34] BM Add MS 12404, 405, Edward Long's notes for his "History of Jamaica." Also *HC Sess Pap* 1790(698)LXXXVII, 311 and 334. These estimates exclude the cost of provisions grown on the estate.
[35] Ullrich B. Phillips, "A Jamaica Slave Plantation," *American Historical Review*, XIX (April 1914), 544.
[36] As the soil became exhausted with age and constant use, the number of laborers per acre had to be increased to obtain the same yield as before.

INTRODUCTION 13

up to cultivation by ambitious planters, often with extensive capital investments and no time to lose. Large consignments of new Africans were imported and put to work clearing land (the hardest, most unhealthy work of all), often without any period of seasoning. Those remaining alive after the first planting maintained the estate until the first harvest (about 1½ years later), when another herd of newcomers arrived. The virgin estates took a heavy toll of lives. When it is recalled that Dominica, St. Vincent, Tobago, and Grenada were all added to the Crown and opened to British cultivators in 1763, it is understandable that the slave trade should have reached its zenith during the ten years which followed.

Much of the debt accumulated by British planters between 1763 and 1807 came from stocking new colonies, and unsettled portions of old ones, with slaves.[37] "The purchase of new negroes," wrote Edward Long of Jamaica, "is the most chargeable article attending these estates, and the true source of distress, under which the owners suffer."[38] Because West Indian agriculture still depended on hand labor, the volume of production was directly related to the number of Negro slaves. Thus the purchase of slaves had to be continued even when profits declined.

As British West Indian estates began to lose money they were mortgaged in bits and pieces to local and overseas creditors. Pensions, annuities, and title inaccuracies were often concealed. Promises of financial reform were lightly made and too seldom kept. Recovering bad debts was frustrating if not impossible in the local law courts. All creditors could hope for was a long period of exceptionally high prices for West Indian produce.

The London sugar factors were the only investors still willing and able to grant considerable amounts of credit to West Indian proprietors. Many factors were themselves planters and, knowing the business from both ends, could draw up reasonably secure mortgage deeds. Moreover, the fact that merchants sold

[37]Sheridan, "Organization of the Slave Trade," 258.
[38]Quoted by Thomas Clarkson, *An Essay on the Impolicy of the Slave Trade* (London 1788), 99, probably from Long's *History of Jamaica* (1774).

sugar on commission, and acted as agents for the planters' private concerns, ensured some degree of cooperation. This was true not only because the relationship demanded integrity and mutual confidence, but because the factor had legal aid:

> At some time before the end of the eighteenth century, the courts in England appear to have ruled that a factor who had effects of the planters in his hands could pay himself what they owed him without their special order, but could not pay a debt to anyone else without it. Thus, so long as the sugars continued to reach the factor's hands, they afforded him not only a commission, but a security....[39]

Stock on hand, however, was not much security for the debts incurred by 1788. In the books of John Pinney of Bristol, a proprietor turned factor, the floating debt usually amounted to something between £20,000 and £30,000, while another £100,000 or more was secured by formal mortgages.[40] The whole British West Indian liability in 1788 was £20 million sterling, and even with an annual profit of 4% on that year's gross sales of £3,867,266 as a guideline, the planters could not repay the amount for well over a century.[41] Their position was already hopeless.

One fact about this debt tied it irrevocably to the question of abolition. Because sugar production was variable, and because the land itself was useless without laborers, mortgages and other West Indian credits were usually granted on the security

[39] Pares, *Merchants and Planters*, 48. This rule was confirmed during the sugar crisis of 1799, when factors obtained loans from the Bank of England on the security of their clients' sugar; but it seems to have been accepted practice before that. Cf. "Minutes of the Subcommittee of West India Merchants appointed in 1799", West India Committee Archives, London.

[40] Pares, *A West India Fortune*, 177–178.

[41] £20 million is the estimate of George Hibbert, a prominent West India merchant, in *HC Sess Pap* 1790(698)LXXXVII, 388. Gross sales were based on all West Indian produce imported into Great Britain, *PC Rpt 1789*, part IV, #10.

INTRODUCTION 15

of the slaves themselves,[42] whose depreciation could be offset by fresh imports as long as there was a British slave trade.

In summary, these points seem valid for the period 1784–1789, when the abolition campaign began:

1. The greater part of the British slave trade was concentrated in the hands of a few large Liverpool firms whose connections with the West Indian economy were neither direct nor extensive.
2. The primary markets for the British-carried slaves were the non-British colonies of the Caribbean.
3. British merchants were facing increased competition from foreigners, chiefly the French, in the slave trade to the non-British colonies.
4. Living and working conditions in the West Indies made necessary a constant importation of new slaves to keep up the labor force, compensate for soil depletion, and clear new land for cultivation.
5. Increasing costs, financial imprudence, and the recurring need to purchase slaves had reduced plantation profits and had thrown West Indian proprietors deeply into debt to their factors in England.
6. A considerable number of people in Great Britain were directly or indirectly dependent for their living on West Indian enterprises, whose continued success was believed to depend on the supply of African slaves.

[42]Pares, *A West India Fortune,* 279, and *HC Sess Pap* 1790(698)LXXXVII, 388. Sheridan ("Organization of the Slave Trade," 262) quotes the testimony of West India merchant James Baillie, that many planters entered into agreements with their creditors to keep up the number of slaves, and hence the value, of the mortgaged estates.

2

The Defenders of the Slave Trade

Very early in the 18th century West Indian planters and merchants had organized into committees, clubs, and societies, which carefully exploited the widespread financial and imperial interest in the West Indies. Individual proprietors, retiring with their fortunes to England, set themselves up as country gentlemen and cultivated the parliamentary interest that accrued with their newly-purchased estates. In time, through their efforts, there grew up images of the West Indies as the most valuable possessions of the Empire, and of "West Indians" as men of vast wealth and an ostentatious style of living. Thus, although their economic position was slowly deteriorating, the West Indian planters and merchants remained politically influential all through the latter half of the century.

The image of opulence was only partly true. "West Indians" known in society were a small, largely interrelated group of absentee planters who had grown up in the Caribbean and still had many connections there. They were indeed rich, and lived accordingly: "the Beeston Long mansion in Bishopsgate Street . . . and the Robert Hibbert residence just beyond the city, were noted for the refined splendor of their appointments." Further out, near Carshalton in Surrey, Samuel Long, Beeston's brother, owned an estate spread over two square miles, including a spacious mansion surrounded by formal gardens.[1] Behind this glittering facade, which lasted through the 1790's, was a much larger group of men with West Indian interests who occupied financial, political, and official administrative positions in the kingdom. They were merchants, lawyers, annuitants, creditors, heirs and husbands of heiresses, ranging from Dukes to petty tradesmen. Few had ever seen the West Indies. A good example was John Nesbitt, a West India merchant who inherited estates and an electoral interest in Winchelsea, and sugar estates in Jamaica and Grenada. He had himself elected for Winchelsea in 1780 and 1784 and was active in opposition to William Pitt.[2] Nesbitt conformed to the image of the West Indian by living a high life and by losing his fortune. Clement Tudway, another absentee, was more prudent. Inheriting from his father a long-established Antigua property as well as a strong political interest at Wells, Tudway sat for that constituency from 1761 to 1815.

In the Parliament that met from 1784 to 1790, there were nine "West Indians" and at least thirty-six other members with West Indian interests. Financially and socially they were much divided. But on questions affecting the West Indies they voted together, making one of the strongest interest groups of their time.

Generally they tended to support Pitt's administration. London merchants trading to the Caribbean were inclined to co-operate with every government in power. West Indians who styled themselves country gentlemen tended to follow the line of cautious independence for which that class was well known. Although few of them could carry the House by their oratory, their silent, usually dependable votes were much valued by a

[1] Ragatz, *Absentee Landlordism*, 10; "A Survey of Estates belonging to Samuel Long, Esq. . . . taken in 1788 and 1790." MS roll in the Surrey Collection, Croydon Central Library.
[2] Information on M. P.'s unless otherwise noted comes from Sir Lewis Namier and John Brooke, *The House of Commons, 1754–1790*, (3 vols., London, 1964), and from the *Dictionary of National Biography*.

minister who legislated by acquiescence more than by command.

One of the more capable West Indians in Parliament was Sir William Young. He deserves notice as the gradually recognized spokesman for moderate West Indian opinion and as the author of the only constructive attempt to defeat abolition. An absentee planter and a "firm supporter of Pitt", Sir William sat from 1784 to 1806 for St. Mawes, Cornwall, in the Marquis of Buckingham's interest, and thereafter for Buckingham town. In 1782 Young had been delegated by the proprietors of Tobago to represent their interests in the peace negotiations with France. A historian of sorts and a Fellow of the Royal Society, he was also Secretary to the Association for Promoting the Discovery of the Interior Parts of Africa. His property in St. Vincent's was considerable[3] and in 1794 he was appointed co-agent for that island. On the floor of the House he spoke rapidly and sometimes indistinctly; in committees he was much more effective.

Outside Parliament, West Indian interests were represented by organizations in London, Bristol, and Liverpool. The two in London were naturally predominant, for the capital was not only the center of colonial administration but at once the greatest source of credit and the chief depot for West Indian produce. London prices influenced the whole British sugar market. Absentee planters tended to settle there, and outport merchants kept branch offices in "the City".[4]

The Society of West India Merchants was the older of the two London bodies. The Merchants' minute-books begin in April 1769, but there is every reason to believe some kind of organization, however loose or temporary, existed before then. The Society handled much of the organization of the West

[3] According to the Report of the St. Vincent's Assembly (CO 261:9, 116) he lost more than £19,000 in the Carib rebellion of 1795 but remained quite solvent.
[4] John Pinney, a West India merchant from Bristol, had to visit London several times each month; his son managed the business there for a time. Cf. Pinney Papers, Family letter-book #8, Bristol University Library.

Indian trade, agreed on prices of produce, entered into formal agreements with shipowners other than themselves, and settled wage scales with the wharfingers at the London docks. It also arranged convoys for the West India sugar fleets in wartime. In the 1790's the Merchants initiated the establishment of the Thames Police and the construction of the West India docks. Until colonial agents were appointed around 1778, they also served as an informal channel of communication between the government and the colonial legislatures.

West Indian planters had established their own society or club, probably earlier than the merchants. Its functions were as much social as political. On January 18, 1775, a general meeting of both planters and merchants took place to discuss the crisis in the American colonies. A coalition seemed valuable to both sides, and after a series of similar joint meetings a Standing Committee of Planters and Merchants was formed on April 29, 1778. Its organization was similar to that of the Society of Merchants, and it made use of the same secretary and treasurer. Increasingly, however, the Standing Committee took over the political and liaison functions of the Merchants and became an important body in its own right. From May 1785 it began to keep separate records. Its chairman, until his death in 1808, was Lord Penrhyn, M. P. for Liverpool 1784–1790.[5]

There were a few differences in membership between the two groups. The Society of Merchants was the more professional and admittance to its ranks was often (if not always) gained by nomination from an established member. The Standing Committee was essentially a group of delegates elected at a general meeting of planters and merchants or co-opted from time to time. During the period 1788–1807 about 106 members were assigned to it, though only 30–60 attended any one meeting. Many of these belonged, of course, to the Society of Mer-

[5]The development of the London societies is described in Lillian M. Penson, "The West India Interest in the Eighteenth Century," *English Historical Review*, XXXVIII; and by Ragatz, *Fall of the Planter Class*, 94–96.

chants as well. All planters and merchants were invited to general meetings called by the Standing Committee; sometimes annuitants, mortgagees, and other creditors came as well. It will be noticed that the West India merchants could thus launch a double-barrelled attack on Government measures inimical to their interests. In fact, formal communications between the two organizations, sometimes published for their propaganda value, were often written and received by the same persons.

The treasury of the Merchants' Society was augmented when necessary by voluntary contributions from members. The Standing Committee, on the other hand, was financed by a general levy on planters called the "trade rate" or simply "trade", which ranged from a penny to a shilling per hundredweight of sugar, puncheon of rum, or thousand pounds of coffee. The trade rate was fixed for definite periods, usually a year or two, at general meetings. It was levied on all West Indian produce entering London (the outport societies collected their own "trade") so that most West Indian producers, large or small, had to contribute. London factors entered the amount in their books alongside freight, insurance, and commission charges, but did not always pass it along to the Standing Committee, whose accounts were usually in arrears.

The Standing Committee and the Merchants' Society were not chartered companies. They had no recognized set of rules and no legal rights. But because of their longstanding influence in commercial, financial, and political circles, they were consulted by the government of the day on all measures pertaining to the West Indies and to the marketing of West Indian produce. Since the 1730's they had had an enviable record of success in protecting their own interests.

In particular, the collective opinion of the 120-odd members of the Merchants' Society (and of the surprising number of "planters" represented by the Standing Committee who were primarily merchants of one sort or another) carried weight with Pitt's trade-conscious administration. A brief investigation will reveal why this was so.

During the 18th century each new group of Treasury officials took pains to forge personal links with the moneyed interest in the "City" in order to ensure the success of their legislative programs.[6] Relations between the two became very close. Merchants and bankers were willing to cooperate with any administration not openly hostile to their interests, and over the years they built up considerable influence respecting both purely financial matters and related issues. About abolition, which was primarily a commercial question, they would have much to say.

"The City's" communications with Government passed largely through the hands of the directors of merchant trading companies, of banking and insurance groups, and of the two great credit organizations, the Bank of England and the South Sea Company. A significant number of these directors had West Indian property or business concerns, as shown by their membership in the London West India societies. Those listed in the London directories between 1788 and 1807 included three consuls and a governor of the Russia Company, a governor of the Eastland Co. and a deputy governor of the Levant Co., two commissioners of the Hudson's Bay Company, at least three directors of the South Sea Co., four more of the East India Co. and six of the Royal Exchange Assurance Office. Half the governing committee of the Africa Company also belonged to the West Indian societies.

The Bank of England was especially important as a touchstone of government finance. In each year of the period here considered from four to eight of its twenty-odd directors were West Indian merchants. Two or possibly three served as Governor. The list for 1788, when abolition was first introduced to Parliament, included these directors: Beeston Long, head of an extensive Jamaica-based family, and chairman of the West India Merchants' Society; Richard Neave, Long's alternate as chair-

[6]See Lucy Sutherland, "The City of London in Eighteenth-Century Politics", in R. Pares and A.J.P. Taylor, eds., *Essays Presented to Sir Lewis Namier* (London, 1956), 51–53.

man, who ran "one of the first Houses in the City of London" and collected sugar estates as a sideline;[7] Peter Isaac Thellusson, the enterprising son of a vastly rich sugar factor;[8] Godfrey Thornton, a member of the Standing Committee of Planters and Merchants, Governor of the Bank in 1794–95; Samuel Bosanquet, whose brother Charles was a leader in both West Indian groups; and Brook Watson, an active opponent of abolition in the parliamentary debates of 1788–1790. One other director, William Snell, may also have had West Indian connections.

Caribbean agriculture and commerce required so much capital and credit that many factors slipped easily into banking practices. Such were John and Alexander Anderson of Philpot Lane, and Thomas and Samuel Boddington, mentioned frequently in the correspondence of John Pinney of Bristol.

Considering their connections within "the City", it is not surprising that several West Indians became alderman of London. John Anderson, mentioned above, was one, colonial agent George Hibbert another. Generally the London aldermen were well known to the sugar merchants and could be relied upon to look after their interests. Brook Watson, Nathaniel Newnham, and William Ewer, apparently unconnected with Africa or the West Indies, presented anti-abolition petitions from the London merchants to Parliament. They followed an old custom.[9]

Altogether the West Indian interest was well situated to tap an important reservoir of public opinion, either by means of the recognized authority of its adherents or simply by talking around the "City", publicly or privately, as much as possible. That they used their position in defense of the slave trade cannot be doubted. But nothing can show what effect they had, for the London business world would probably have opposed abolition as a matter of course.

[7] CO 296:4, 43, Lord Hobart to Governor Picton of Trinidad, June 1801.
[8] Thellusson's father died in 1797, leaving over £700,000 to various members of his family. Cf. *Dictionary of National Biography*.
[9] Lillian Penson, *The Colonial Agents of the British West Indies* (London, 1924), 228.

Treasury officials, in any event, needed no convincing. One of the Joint Secretaries was George Rose, an expert on trade matters.[10] In right of his wife, the heiress of an Antigua proprietor, he owned several sugar estates; and he may also have been agent for Dominica.[11] In spite of his close friendship with William Pitt, Rose opposed immediate abolition right from the start. The other Joint Secretary was Charles Long, Beeston's brother, a member of the Society of Planters and Merchants.

With men like Rose and Long at the Treasury and with West Indian landowners prominent in the great credit and trading concerns, the case for abolition could not have received a sympathetic hearing in the City of London. What about the merchants who sat in the House of Commons? There were just over sixty of them in 1788, the majority in business in London. Most were engaged in large-scale dealings which brought them into close contact with Government.[12] In the absence of evidence other than the opinions of abolitionist historians, it can only be suggested that the merchants in the House were as susceptible to West Indian influence as those in the City of London.

The West Indian interest so far described was "officially unofficial." Strictly speaking, none of the company directors, Treasury officials, or members of Parliament obtained their posts because of their West Indian possessions. This did not prevent them from using their positions to further the interests of the islands, but they were discrete and left few records.

A few men paid to work behind the scenes for the benefit of the West Indies did leave records. These were the colonial agents. Elected by the proprietors or appointed by Royal War-

[10]In 1793 Rose wrote *A Brief Examination into the Increase of the Revenue, Commerce, and Manufacture of Great Britain since the Peace of 1783*, a defense of the navigation laws; it passed through seven editions.
[11]Rose never mentioned his agency, but is listed for the period 1784–1805 in Penson, *Colonial Agents*, appendix II, 250–254. In May 1785 he introduced the Dominica Free Port Bill to Parliament, normally the agent's duty.
[12]Namier and Brooke, *History of Parliament*, I, 131–5.

rant, each agent acted as attorney for his colony in all its legal proceedings in England. He consulted with the appropriate officials regarding new legislation, administrative problems, or appointments to office, and he supplied both Government and colony with valuable information. Whenever bills relevant to his island or to the West Indies in general came before Parliament the agent was expected to transmit petitions, coordinate support or opposition, try to influence the officials and M. P.'s concerned, and report fully to the corresponding committee of the colonial legislature. Many of the agents' functions were paralleled on a general scale by the Society of Planters and Merchants, to which they belonged ex-officio. But whereas the Society kept rather vague records, the agents' reports and correspondence are detailed and often revealing. They tell much about the defense of the slave trade.

All the agents were resident in or near London after 1786. They were men of some standing, wealthy merchants or government officials and some sat in Parliament. George Rose and Sir William Young have already been introduced. Sir William's co-agent, Sir William Manning, was a West Indian merchant and Member of Parliament. From 1763 to 1792 Barbados' agent was Samuel Estwick, a political pamphleteer who sat for Westbury in Wiltshire.[13] A later agent who warrants a special note was George Chalmers of the Bahamas. Like the proprietors he represented after 1792, Chalmers was an American loyalist who had grown up in a slave-holding community and loathed any kind of philanthropy associated with "natural rights" and "laws of mankind". He hated Wilberforce all his life.[14] Chalmers performed the duties of agent before he received the title, but that was only half his work. He was also employed as chief clerk to Lord Hawkesbury at the Privy Council Committee for Trade and Plantations. His desk was conveniently placed be-

[13] Estwick and John Stanley, who was returned for Hastings in 1784 while still agent for Nevis, should be added to Namier and Brooke's list (*History of Parliament*, I, 161) of agents in Parliament from 1754 to 1790.
[14] G. A. Cockcroft, *The Public Life of George Chalmers* (New York 1939), 99.

tween the Privy Council office and the Home Secretary's office (which had charge of colonial administration) so that he might act as a liaison in the normal course of colonial business.[15] In 1788, when Lord Hawkesbury was asked to investigate the slave trade as a prelude to its abolition, he turned to Chalmers for help.

Agents, officials, M. P.'s, and merchants: the London West Indian interest was so widespread, so well organized, and so powerfully represented in Government that it needed little assistance to defend the slave trade. It was otherwise in the outports. There were West Indian organizations in Bristol, Liverpool, Greenock, Glasgow, and a few other ports. But they were uniformly small, poor, and politically ineffective. Only the first two responded to the threat of abolition, and they had to seek outside help. They and their allies will be mentioned here as contrasts to the London organizations, and then for the most part ignored.

Bristol served a growing inland market for sugar and coffee but her West Indian merchants did not, apparently, operate on a large scale. They were poorly organized. The "New West India Society" which appeared after the American war never had more than a dozen members and spent its small revenues on monthly social dinners at a local coffee house. Generally it was content to follow the lead of the London Standing Committee, for as the members wrote to James Tobin, their self-appointed agent in the capital: "If the Gentlemen in London should decline any interference in the business, it is much to be feared that an application from hence will have very little weight."[16]

Although some of the Bristol sugar factors owned property in the islands, they rarely discussed issues related to it. Their primary concern was with local trade conditions and they preferred to work through the Society of Merchant Venturers. The Venturers, although similarly unenthusiastic and poor, were

[15]Penson, *Colonial Agents*, 235.
[16]Minutes of the New West India Society, April 9, 1789. Tobin was a partner of John Pinney for many years.

a larger and more respected organization with a semi-official status recognized by the Privy Council Committee for Trade. Therefore most of the petitions and delegations sent to London in defense of the slave trade came from the Venturers and not from the West India Society.

The West India Club in Liverpool was even more obscure than that of Bristol, since most of the trade was to Africa and America.[17] What little produce came in from the West Indies was usually brought by slave merchants, who had their own rough organization. As in Bristol, the defense of the slave trade settled in the hands of the most official and respectable body: in Liverpool, the Mayor and Common Council. The Council was a self-perpetuating body which co-opted new members as needed, and over the years it had come to be dominated by the African merchants. Even the Mayor was often a slave trader. In addition, Mayor and Council were ex-officio trustees of the Liverpool docks, responsible in principle for their growing revenues to the residents of the city.[18] Thus the African merchants were able to initiate petitions, or send delegations, in three separate capacities, a position they used to the utmost to combat abolition.

Because of the distance from Liverpool and Bristol to the center of legislative activity at Westminster, the day-to-day work of opposing abolition fell mainly to the members of Parliament: for Bristol, Lord Sheffield and Matthew Brickdale; for Liverpool, Banastre Tarleton and the brothers Gascoyne.

John Holroyd, Baron Sheffield in the Irish peerage, was a leading authority on commerce and agriculture and a prolific writer of political pamphlets. As a champion of the navigation laws,[19]

---

[17] I have been unable to find any records of the Liverpool West India Club for the 18th century, except for a few letters written to its Bristol counterpart, asking for help in defending the slave trade.

[18] J. A. Picton, *Memorials of Liverpool, Historical and Topographical* (2 vols., Liverpool, 1907), I, 225 ff. Cf. Petitions from the Mayor and Council in the *House of Commons Journals* for May 20, 1789 and March 14, 1796.

[19] It is significant that most of the non-West Indian supporters of the slave trade, like Lord Sheffield, were determined to keep the Navigation

he supported both the African and West Indian trades. Successive marriages to the daughters of Thomas Pelham and Lord North assured his rise in society, while his reputation for knowledge and hard work grew in the House of Commons. Altogether, he was a powerful enemy for Wilberforce to cope with.

Bristol's second member, Matthew Brickdale, had retired at the age of thirty-four when his father died leaving him a fortune said to be £100,000. He was first elected in 1768, lost his seat during the American War, then sat again from 1780 to 1790. He owned no West Indian property as far as is known, and followed an irregular political line. But he was a constant supporter of Bristol commercial interests in the Commons.

Banastre Tarleton was elected as a Foxite by the freemen of Liverpool largely on the strength of his brutally heroic record in the American War. In 1787 he published a boastful "History of the Campaigns of 1780 and 1781 in the Southern Provinces of North America" which cast such discredit on his superior officers that Tarleton lost his chance for further promotion. Loquacious, strong-minded, passably educated and well-known in society, an outspoken Whig and a friend of the Prince of Wales, Tarleton could have been a formidable parliamentary figure. But his tendency to hyperbolic generalization, useful perhaps to a working cavalry colonel, was not successful in the House of Commons, and no amount of repetition could make it so. His frequent outbursts against abolition (except when written beforehand by his mistress, the authoress Mary Robinson) helped lower the tone of the whole debate.[20]

Tarleton is the M. P. most closely associated with the defense of the slave trade because he sat for Liverpool from 1790 to 1806, when the abolition question was at its height. His pre-

---

laws intact after the American Revolution. When the West Indians succeeded in amending those laws in 1806, at the expense of British merchants, they lost the favor of valuable allies in the fight against abolition.

[20]For information about Tarleton and "Perdita" Robinson see the exhaustive biography by Robert D. Bass, *The Green Dragoon* (London, 1957).

decessor, however, was equally important. Richard Pennant, Baron Penrhyn of Ireland, came from a family with extensive West Indian connections. He had been in Parliament since 1761 and was well-known in politics. In 1784 he defeated Tarleton by a mere thirteen votes; but in 1790, thinking that his alliance with Bamber Gascoyne ensured his election, he cut off the supply of free ale to the citizens of Liverpool and in the ensuing uproar lost his seat.[21] Thereafter he devoted himself to the chairmanship of the Standing Committee of Planters and Merchants, in London.

The second seat at Liverpool was controlled by the Mayor and Council in the government interest. Bamber Gascoyne held it from 1780 to 1796; his brother Isaac succeeded him and sat until 1831. Their father, the only son of a Lord Mayor of London, had made a small fortune as Receiver-General of the Customs and a Lord Commissioner of the Admiralty.[22] He also had gained, through marriage and inheritance, a number of West Indian estates which passed to his elder son and namesake, Bamber, when he died in 1791. Bamber Gascoyne was never very popular, and when he inherited the family businesses his brother Isaac took over his seat in Parliament. Isaac was generally considered a commonplace orator, a man of little knowledge and of poor judgment. But he was an eager and active member of the House, useful to Liverpool, and he had a first-class election manager. Backed by the Common Council and his own family interest, he had small need to win fame at Westminster. Both Isaac and Bamber Gascoyne were "conservative to the backbone" and uniformly supported the measures of Government.[23]

Such were the defenders of the slave trade. As a cross-section of the business and landed community of their time, they were no better and no worse than their opponents. It would be helpful to forget, for a moment, the very name of "West Indians", which has been so much maligned and distorted by abolitionists

[21] J. A. Picton, *Memorials of Liverpool*, I, 258–259.
[22] *Ibid.*, 247.
[23] *Ibid.*, 42, 272.

and their historians, and to picture instead a large, mixed group of businessmen-landowners who derived part or all of their income from growing or marketing colonial produce. Allied to this group were a small number of merchants who followed a distasteful but legitimate and hitherto necessary trade. All of them, in one way or another, were men of business; and it was chiefly to other men of business that they appealed, when that "necessary trade" was threatened with abolition.

The merchants and planters described in this chapter considered themselves, and were considered, highly respectable. It is difficult, at this distance in time, to put oneself in their place, and to see the abolition campaign through their eyes. Perhaps the closest parallel in modern times would be the medical researcher's view of the anti-vivisectionist league; and if that confrontation between moral anguish and the necessities of social progress is kept in mind, it may be possible to understand why the West Indians reacted with such indignation to the attack launched, almost without warning, on their means of livelihood and on their character, in the public arena of Parliament.

3

Prelude to Abolition

No one can hope to understand Parliament's stubborn resistance to abolition, or the arguments used to support it, without first considering the circumstances in which they appeared. The period of study, 1784–1807, falls roughly into three parts— several years of vague, unorganized argument, a short interval of objective, official investigation, and the dramatic outbreak of parliamentary debate.

The question of abolition was not new in 1788. A series of pamphlets directed against the slave system had led to legal action even before the American revolution. Lord Mansfield's decision of 1770, declaring slavery illegal in Great Britain, was the result. If, as Reginald Coupland suggested,[1] anti-slavery feeling was first aroused by the appearance in England of absentee planters and their household slaves, then Mansfield's decision actually hindered the progress of the movement by confining slavery to the far-away West Indies, of whose internal life the British public was only vaguely informed. There was no immediate attempt to extend the anti-slavery law to the

[1]R. Coupland, "The British Anti-Slavery Movement" in *The Cambridge History of the British Empire*, II, 191.

colonies, and the volume of public discussion declined over the next decade.

A strong undercurrent of hostility to slavery remained which rose to the surface on several occasions. Edward Long mentioned it when introducing his *History of Jamaica* in 1774:[2]

> When the planters have complained of violations done to their liberty, the enemies of the West India islands have often retorted upon them the impropriety of their clamouring with so much vehemence for what they deny to so many thousand Negroes, whom they held in bondage.

In his answer to such enemies, Long compared the West Indian planters to the ancient Greeks, who were slave-owners and yet champions of freedom. Generally, he maintained, the master of slaves is one of the most liberal of men.

The occasional nature of the argument indicates that neither side really expected anything conclusive to come of it. At the time Long wrote, the West Indies were still prosperous and their influence in Parliament was clear. Moreover, they were allied with the slave-holding colonies on the American mainland, whose hostility to interference from the mother country was already aroused.[3] In short, almost nothing could be done

---

[2] Edward Long, *The History of Jamaica, or General Survey of the Antient and modern State of that Island* (3 vols. London, 1774), I, 5.

[3] It has been maintained in several surveys of the anti-slavery movement that David Hartley proposed abolition to Parliament in 1775. In fact, he was searching for a means of establishing Parliament's right to legislate for America, without making a direct claim. He proposed to send an act, to be passed by each colonial legislature, "That every slave in North America should be entitled to his trial by jury in all criminal cases." If the act were accepted, each colony might then adopt measures gradually to abolish slavery. Hartley's motion is similar to one made by the West Indians in 1797; and his cautious arguments parallel those used in defense of the slave trade: "It would be infinitely absurd to send over to America an act to abolish slavery at one word, because however repugnant the practice may be to the laws of morality or policy, yet to expel an evil which has spread so far, and which has been suffered for such a length of time, requires information of facts and circumstances, and the greatest discretion to root it out...." *The Parliamentary Register, or History of the Proceedings and Debates in the House of Commons*, III, 264–265.

by the English about slavery in America, and the abolitionists knew it.

The American revolution was therefore of critical importance to the abolition movement. As a result of the revolutionary war, the West Indies lost not only their strongest allies but their own economic and military security in addition. Ruined by famine and fighting, and deprived of a valuable market for rum and molasses as well as a source of supplies, they were forced to cling to the mother country for protection. The Order-in-Council of 1783, which banned American shipping from the British West Indies, made their dependence permanent and left them vulnerable to the attacks of their critics; while the loss of the mainland colonies occasioned a re-assessment of Empire, in which West Indian agriculture figured prominently.

Trouble began immediately after the war. James Ramsay, returned to England after nineteen years as a clergyman on St. Kitt's, published an essay which bitterly attacked the treatment of West Indian slaves and the character of their masters.[4] Ramsay was probably not an innocent observer, but his indignation and detailed reporting impressed the public. It also enraged West Indians and set the tone of their defense for years to come. The unfortunate Ramsay was simply hounded to death. His past life and character were vilified in pamphlet after pamphlet. Old friends deserted him and when he tried to seclude himself in the vicarage of Teston in Kent, he was followed by threats and whispering campaigns. When he died in 1789, Crisp Molyneux, West Indian M. P. for Lynn, told his son: "Ramsay is dead—I have killed him!"[5]

A second important pamphlet was differently, but no more creditably, opposed by the slave-trading community. Thomas Clarkson's *Essay on the Slavery and Commerce of the Human Species, Particularly the African*, published in 1786, based on his prize-winning Oxford dissertation, relied on arguments

[4] James Ramsay, *An Essay on the Treatment and Conversion of African Slaves in the British Sugar Colonies* (London, 1784).
[5] *Life of Wilberforce*, I, 235.

deduced from general principles of natural law and natural religion, freely interpreted by the author. The *Essay* was not personally vindictive, but theoretical, almost dogmatic. It drew a similar reply. The "Reverend Raymond Harris" of Liverpool set forth the premise that whatever practices were mentioned in the Bible without condemnation were sanctioned by God for all time. Then he simply culled examples of slavery from the Old Testament to conclude that slavery, and hence the slave trade, was part of the Christian heritage.[6]

Unfortunately for this effort, the Evangelical and Methodist abolitionists were old hands at quoting the Bible; half a dozen replies were off the press in a fortnight. Moreover, Harris himself was exposed as one Don Raymondo Hormaza, an ex-Jesuit from Spain, currently under suspension by the Roman Catholic bishop of Liverpool for irregular behavior.[7] Considering the state of public opinion on Spanish Jesuits at that time, Harris probably did the slave trade more harm than good. But he was presented with a reward by the Corporation of Liverpool.

Harris's pamphlet was almost the only public defense made before abolition was taken up in Parliament. The slave trade interests could not (or would not) compete in terms of morality and natural law, and there was as yet no concrete proposal to argue against. Indeed, if the abolitionist pamphlets of this period are separated from developments over the next fifty years, and viewed in the wide context of contemporary national life, there is no reason to consider them significant. To the West Indian planters they were a nuisance and nothing more.

It came as a considerable surprise, therefore, when early in 1788 William Pitt instituted a full investigation of the slave

[6]Rev. Raymond Harris, *Scriptural Researches on the Licitness of the Slave Trade, showing its conformity with the principles of Natural and revealed religion, delineated in the sacred writings of the Word of God.* (Liverpool, March 1788).

[7]He may have been working in the slave trade for the Spanish government. An account of him was sent by William Walton of Liverpool to Lord Hawkesbury (BM Add MS 38416, 24–30) part of which is printed in Elizabeth Donnan, *Documents Illustrating the History of the Slave Trade to America* (4 vols., London, 1928), II, 577.

trade by the Privy Council Committee for Trade and Plantations.[8]

Pitt's motives are clear. Having induced his friend Wilberforce to take up a parliamentary campaign for abolition,[9] he wanted, as usual, to obtain as much information on the subject as possible. He may also have hoped that the Privy Council's authority would lend support to a bill which he knew could not be a Government measure.

In any event Pitt chose the best possible man for the job. The Privy Council Committee for Trade contained twenty-one members, but it was the president, Lord Hawkesbury, who in fact directed policy. As Charles Jenkinson, he had attached himself to Bute and then North, earning a reputation for loyalty and shrewd management. He was even more of a "King's Friend" than that epithet usually suggests, as the authors of *The Rolliad* grudgingly admitted:[10]

> K---: Jenky, I own divides my heart,
> Skill'd in each deep and secret art
> To keep my C–mm–ns down;
> His views, his principles are mine;
> For these I'd willingly resign
> My Kingdom and my Crown.

Despite a "total lack of personal charm"[11] Jenkinson moved rapidly up the administrative ladder, receiving several lucrative sinecures along the way. In 1786 he was created Baron Hawkesbury and appointed President of the newly-organized Privy Council Committee for Trade. At that post, "his efficiency

[8] The Order of Reference was issued February 11. The Privy Council Committee was coming to be known as the Board of Trade, but the former name will be used in this account to avoid confusion of terms.
[9] It would be interesting to know if Pitt asked Wilberforce to introduce abolition merely to keep the latter in Parliament where his independent support was always helpful. Certainly he did not bargain for the kind of crusade that Wilberforce developed.
[10] *The Rolliad* (22nd edition, London, 1812), 442.
[11] R. Pares, *King George III and the Politicians* (Oxford, 1953), 12.

and enormous capacity for methodical hard work rapidly made him the virtual dictator of British commercial policy overseas."[12] He was, above all else, disinterested; and Pitt rightly depended on him for a fair report on the slave trade.

Now to call any English administrator of the 1790's "disinterested" or "objective" may seem näive. But Hawkesbury's conduct of the slave trade enquiry was both. On January 29, 1788 he received an appeal from Stephen Fuller, agent for Jamaica, to convince the King of the necessity of ordering the West Indian governors to guard against unrest and rebellion among the slaves while abolition was being discussed.[13] Hawkesbury sent all the papers to Pitt with a note asking for a conference, and on the latter's advice told Fuller to apply directly to Lord Sydney at the Home Office. On the surface this transaction seems quite ordinary. But Hawkesbury had been making his own enquiries since the previous October[14] and knew that Fuller was trying to implicate him as a defender of the slave trade while alarming the public with warnings of slave rebellion.[15]

Hawkesbury set his clerks to work as soon as the Order of Reference was published. Copies were made of all relevant petitions sent to the House of Commons. Reports and statistics were solicited from the Committee of African Merchants and the Society for Propagating the Gospel. Sir George Yonge of the War Department was asked about deaths among West India troops and the space allowed them aboard military transport ships. Hawkesbury even sent Raymond Harris's scriptural defense of slavery to the Bishop of Llandaff, asking for a careful criticism of its principles. Nothing was being taken for granted.[16]

---

[12] A. M. McC. Madden, "The Imperial Machinery of the Younger Pitt" in H. R. Trevor-Roper, ed., *Essays in British History presented to Sir Keith Feiling* (London, 1961), 179.
[13] BM Add MS 38416, 6–7.
[14] See, for instance, BM Add 38222, 133.
[15] BM Add MS 38192, 58: Pitt to Hawkesbury, January 30, 1788.
[16] This is only a sample of the first four days' activities. BT 3:1 and 3:2 are full of the letters and orders which poured out of the Committee's office during the following year.

On February 15 the West Indian agents were informed of the Committee's objects, and ordered to send all available information to its office. On the 21st they received a lengthy and detailed questionnaire drawn up by Hawkesbury[17] to facilitate the collation of different reports. This questionnaire was also sent, through the governors, to each of the West Indian legislatures.

Later, through the Foreign Office, orders went out to ambassadors in France, Spain, Holland, Portugal, and Denmark to supply details of the African trade of their host countries, and to trade consuls for returns of sugar prices in continental markets. The ambassador in Warsaw was even asked about the effects of freeing the Polish serfs on the prices of labor and land. Hawkesbury was not satisfied with incomplete or unverified reports, even from these men: William Eden in Paris was asked three times for more papers, while Sir John Hort was requested "to state the sources and authorities from whence you derived the information" on the slave trade of Portugal.[18]

One can only feel sorry for the Committee's clerks, who had to transcribe all these reports. In the end they received a bonus "for their extraordinary Labor and attendance",[19] no doubt well deserved. John Reeves, for instance, found the task of preparing a resumé of all previous parliamentary debates on the slave trade "the severest drudgery I ever underwent."[20]

Pitt had hoped a report would be ready in time for debate in May 1788. He joined the almost daily sittings of the Privy Council Committee whenever possible, and had the evidence sent to him between times. But Hawkesbury's thoroughness, combined with the slow return of colonial and diplomatic reports, extended the period of enquiry to April 1789. Consequently the first debates on the slave trade, in May 1788, were conducted with no real knowledge of their subject, and it took all of Pitt's and Hawkesbury's influence to salvage something from the confusion.

[17]Printed in the front of the PC Rpt 1789. The original, in Hawkesbury's hand, is in BM Add Ms 38416, 217–220.
[18]BT 3:1, 331, Fawkener to Hort, August 30, 1788.
[19]BT 3:2, 27. Cottrell to Rose, January 29, 1789.
[20]BM Add MS 38416, 236. Reeves to Hawkesbury, April 11, 1789.

The Slave Trade Regulating Act of 1788 is usually considered a stopgap measure, of little importance in view of the final abolition, and thus it has been treated lightly by historians. In fact, its progress through Parliament is one of the most revealing episodes in the whole history of abolition. The bill was introduced despite objections from both sides, debated in the absence of Wilberforce, drastically amended in the House of Lords and carried after a dramatic showdown between Pitt and his chief ministers. Yet it was the most successful of all the "abolition" measures and the only one to become law before 1806.

As has been noted, Pitt wished the parliamentary debate on abolition to be based on the report of the Privy Council Committee for Trade. He may have felt relieved when Wilberforce's near-fatal illness prevented the introduction of a bill in 1788. In its place, Pitt moved on May 9 "That this House will, early in the next session of Parliament, proceed to take into consideration the circumstances of the Slave Trade, complained of in the said petitions, and what may be fit to be done thereon." He acknowledged that there were different opinions regarding the need for full prohibition, but he maintained that all agreed something ought to be done. Unfortunately, there was too little time and information at the moment to make any discussion of the question advisable.[21]

Pitt's attempt to avoid premature argument failed. Charles James Fox, who never willingly lost a chance to embarrass his rival even when he agreed with him, immediately rose to question the propriety of seeking advice from the King's ministers (i.e., Hawkesbury) when the truth could be discovered by an investigation in the House, "the table of which had been loaded with petitions from all parts of the kingdom." He would, he said, consider the question only on principles of humanity and justice, and would accept nothing but a total abolition. Those who argued for mere regulation were "dupes of error."[22]

[21]William Cobbett, *The Parliamentary History of England, from the Earliest Period to the Year 1803* (London, reprint by T. C. Hansard, 1812–1820), XXVII, 496–7.
[22]*Ibid.*, 498–500.

Pitt tried to gloss over Fox's emotional attack but the damage had been done. The slave-trading members were willing to ignore moderate criticism but became indignant at anything resembling attacks on their collective character. Lord Penrhyn, who at this time represented Liverpool as well as the London West Indians, replied that he welcomed the enquiry: "the more their conduct was examined, the less they would be found to merit the approbrium with which they had been loaded." And when the charges were proven false, "justice ought to be done to the characters of those who were concerned in it."[23] Bamber Gascoyne echoed the same sentiments.

The House was further upset when Sir William Dolben, who had made his own investigation, recounted in detail the horrors of the "middle passage" across the Atlantic. He dwelt at length on the filthy, poorly ventilated ships, packed so tightly that slaves could hardly stand up, on the appalling frequency of disease and death, and on the wretched condition of the seamen. Rebuttals by Penrhyn and Sir William Young only brought on more criticism. Despite Pitt's third attempt to close the discussion, an immediate enquiry was demanded and Dolben, supported by Thomas Pelham, resolved to bring in a regulating bill.[24]

Everyone seemed concerned to prevent the discussion spreading to the main question of abolition. Dolben deliberately limited his measure to the improvement of conditions on board ships in the Atlantic. He even showed an outline to Gascoyne, Penrhyn, and Matthew Brickdale, who all agreed not to oppose the bill's introduction.[25] When leave was given to bring it in, on May 21, Gascoyne further agreed that an examination of evidence would be undesirable because it would tend to arouse emotions. But on the 23rd, he announced that instructions from his constituents, as well as "mature deliberation" on his own part, compelled him to move the postponement of the bill for three months (in effect, to kill it). Penrhyn, Brickdale,

[23]*Ibid.*, 501.
[24]*Ibid.*, 503–506.
[25]*Parliamentary Register* XXIII, 735.

and Young agreed, although the latter two believed that regulation was desirable after a full investigation was made. There were few members attending that day, and postponement might have been carried. But Sir Charles Middleton, an abolitionist, called for a count of the House and the debate was adjourned for a few days for lack of a quorum.[26]

The way in which Dolben introduced his bill put the opposition at a disadvantage. There had been no specific petition from outside the House on which an enquiry might have been based, so Dolben's own evidence provided the only information for most members. Moreover this was a private member's bill and could pass through its several readings without any evidence allowed against it, unless it was formally opposed on principle.[27] To remedy this defect, Penrhyn and William Ewer[28] presented petitions on the 26th and 28th of May from Liverpool and London Africa merchants "stating the long existence of the slave trade; the essential benefits the country had derived from it; the encouragement that the legislature held out to individuals to embark their fortunes in it; and the injury that they must necessarily suffer from any sudden measure being taken respecting it." Their request to be heard at the Bar of the House was granted.[29]

At this move Sir William Dolben lost his temper, called the petitions an insult to the House, and challenged the slave merchants to prove their assertions by making the trip themselves, preferably in irons. When Penrhyn attempted to restate his position he was crushed by the oratory of Pitt and Fox.

[26]*Ibid.*, 739.
[27]Cf. O. C. Williams, *The Historical Development of Private Bill Procedure and Standing Orders in the House of Commons* (2 vols., London, 1948), I, 26 and 30–33. According to standing orders, no private bill could be introduced without a petition. Dolben apparently got around this by moving "that the House resolve itself into a Committee to consider of the African Slave Trade, as a necessary matter of form, in order that a resolution might be moved in the Committee that the Chairman do ask leave of the House to bring in a bill. . . ." *Parliamentary Register*, XXIII, 735.
[28]William Ewer (c. 1720–1789), M. P. for Dorchester, a London grocer and Levant merchant, director of the Bank of England, 1763–1789.
[29]*Parliamentary Register*, XXIII, 742.

It was not the last time that abolitionists, in a fit of righteous indignation, would condemn a reasonable legal request made by their opponents.

Nevertheless, Penrhyn had won a hearing and the House sat in Committee intermittently from the 2nd to the 17th of June. Five witnesses from Liverpool and one from Bristol appeared for the defense.[30] They tried to prove that there were no unhealthy practices in the African trade, and that the limitations proposed would ruin business. John Tarleton, for instance, produced an extract from his firm's orders to a slave ship captain cautioning him to treat the seamen and slaves with every consideration and to establish a "reign of peace and harmony" on board by a "diffusion of cheerfulness".[31] This part of the testimony was hit hard by abolitionist cross-examination.

The more important task for the House was to discover the optimum number of slaves, in proportion to a ship's tonnage, that would ensure healthy conditions while preserving some profit for the merchants—for overcrowding was generally thought to be the worst abuse. Dolben had originally wanted one man to one ton; John Mathews produced a hypothetical account showing a profit at two men per ton, but a loss for anything less.[32] The other witnesses supported Mathews, of course, but the House disagreed. A survey of Liverpool's slave ships revealed a general average of two men per ton loaded in Africa and 1.9 per ton arriving in the West Indies.[33] Since by Mathew's estimate this proportion yielded a 12% return on investment, it was considered that some reduction could safely be made. Eventually a limit was set at five slaves for every three tons up to 200 tons, and one per ton thereafter. If the slave trade could

[30] John Tarleton, Robert Norris, John Matthews, Archibald Dalzell, and James Penney, delegates appointed by the Liverpool African Committee May 25 (BM Add MS 38416, 93); and James Jones, delegate of the Bristol Merchant Venturers, secretary to the Jamaica Assembly and one of Hawkesbury's early sources of information.

[31] *HC Sess Pap* 1789(633)LXXXII, 48.

[32] *Ibid.*, 21–22. For a criticism of this estimate, see Hyde *et. al.*, "Nature and Profitability of the Slave Trade."

[33] *HC Sess Pap* 1789(633)LXXXII, 5–6.

not be carried on under these regulations, said Pitt, he would retract his previous resolution and bring in immediately a bill for total abolition.[34]

What a marvelous declaration! Suspicious independent members had initiated this bill and given it most of its substance. But while Gascoyne and Penrhyn remained entirely on the defensive, Pitt perceived, expressed, and canalized each new idea that rose from the floor of the House. His declaration was pure bluff, because the end of the session was already overdue, yet it ably expressed the prevailing mood.

While the Liverpool members were still condemning the proportion of slaves per ton allowed, Pitt removed, by casual suggestion, the last obstacle to success in the Commons. A clause in the bill which Pitt either wrote or supported strongly, made all regulations retroactive to June 10. Many members thought it extremely unfair to those ships already outfitted or under way for the African coast. They also believed warnings from Liverpool that until the supply of slaves from the African interior was adjusted to new regulations there would be a surplus of slaves at the coastal stations, which if not sold would be slaughtered by the African dealers.[35] To overcome these scruples, Pitt suggested, immediately after his threat to bring in total abolition, that the House might indemnify or exempt those ships already fitted out for oversized cargoes.[36] No motion was made to that effect, but the bill received its third reading next day without protest.

Lord Penrhyn and Bamber Gascoyne might be excused for spending so much time on the proportion of slaves to tonnage, which was directly related to profits. The abolitionists were equally concerned, for because of the lack of information on other areas of the slave trade at this time, the reduction of

[34] Cobbett, *Parl. Hist.*, XXVII, 598.
[35] Pitt also feared these consequences. He suggested to Grenville on June 29 that Treasury funds might be used to hire additional ships to carry away surplus slaves. Historical Manuscripts Commission, *The Manuscripts of J. B. Fortescue preserved at Dropmore* (10 vols., London, 1892–1927), II, 105. Hereafter cited as *Dropmore MSS*.
[36] Cobbett, *Parl. Hist.*, XXVII, 598.

overcrowding on ships became rather a panacea for all the evils of which they complained. Nor can the Liverpool delegates be blamed for failing to suggest a more sophisticated approach, since they naturally opposed the whole principle of the measure. One wonders, however, at the lack of initiative shown over the retroactive provision of the bill, which was evidently opposed by many moderates. If the slave traders had vigorously pursued Pitt's casual suggestion of indemnities, they might have embarrassed the Prime Minister. The defense was too inflexible for its own good.[37]

As a result of the hasty and one-sided discussion, Dolben's bill was sent to the House of Lords filled with loopholes, contradictions, and vague terminology. Earl Stanhope, a staunch abolitionist, "considered the Bill to be as ill worded, in respect to its clauses, as any Bill ever introduced into that House."[38]

No one was better equipped to offer correctives than Lord Hawkesbury, with five months of investigation already behind him. In his collection of papers on the slave trade there are some ten closely-written pages of observations, criticism, and proposed amendments relating especially to Dolben's bill.[39] The writing is sober, cautious, and thorough, in striking contrast to the Lower House's discussion. Consider Hawkesbury's comments on the proportion of slaves to tonnage. Referring to Sir Charles Middleton's estimate of the minimum space needed by men sleeping in Navy ships, which was more than that allowed to slaves for all purposes, he wrote:[40]

> It is worthy Remark that the Comptroller of the Navy (Middleton) is the grand Umpire who has been constantly referred to during the Discussion of the Bill in both Houses. No other opinion is of any weight. His is the

[37] On the other hand, if the slave traders had been convinced by abolitionist arguments, they would have felt miserable. Psychologically they could not afford to give an inch.
[38] Cobbett, *Parl. Hist.*, XXVII, 642.
[39] BM Add MS 38416, 185–195.
[40] *Ibid.*, 190, "Replies to advocates of abolition."

Criterion by which the operations of an important Branch of Commerce are to be restrained. Now this Gentleman has declared himself, in the Face of the Delegates for Liverpool, to be the Advocate for the Abolition, which he means to effect through this bill.

Then Hawkesbury turned to the figures themselves: the estimate of profits or losses according to various proportions which John Tarleton had sent him from Liverpool, a separate statement of costs provided by James Jones of Bristol, and the records of tonnage and cargoes from previous Liverpool voyages. He filled a half-dozen large folio pages with calculations relating to sleeping space, tonnage, ventilation, and costs. Then, noting that when the merchants' cost estimates were compared to their shipping accounts it appeared that they were operating at a steady loss,[41] he discounted the whole of their evidence and set the rate of profit at £5 per slave, or about 14%. Some reduction in cargoes was therefore possible without ruining the trade. In the end Hawkesbury's schedule of slaves per ton allowed differed only slightly from Dolben's, but the former was accepted by the House of Lords, because it was strongest in point of evidence and argument.[42]

Hawkesbury's continuous criticism of the bill makes it difficult to understand why he finally supported it. Certainly, as one critic has observed, "he had in his make-up no element of self-sacrifice, of idealism, or of far-sighted vision."[43] The defenders of the slave trade looked to him as a friend to their cause, and in view of his later pronouncements their confidence

---

[41] Although his calculations on this point are obscure, Tarleton's account shows a proportion of 1.75 slaves per ton landed in the West Indies, which according to Mathews' figures might be taken as the break-even point. Cf. HC Sess Pap 1789(633)LXXXII, 21 and appendices; and BM Add MS 38416, 204.

[42] That Hawkesbury and not Dolben was the final author of this part of the act is indicated by Hawkesbury's comparison of the several proposed schedules in BM Add MS 38416, 211–212.

[43] Anna L. Linglebach, "The Inception of the British Board of Trade," *American Historical Review*, XXX (July 1925), 727.

seems to have been well placed.⁴⁴ But by June 1788 Hawkesbury had apparently decided that the abuses in the slave trade verified by his own investigation should be stopped, and he knew that proper regulations would not ruin the Liverpool merchants. To make sure the regulations were proper, however, Hawkesbury had to manage Dolben's bill through the House of Lords and sponsor over one hundred amendments of his own.⁴⁵

His support was crucial to the bill's success, for it reassured less knowledgeable peers who hesitated to gratify their humanitarian feelings at the expense of a whole branch of commerce. One of them admitted this frankly in a letter to Hawkesbury:

> My Dear Lord,
> Tho' extremely averse to leave my Proxy, especially upon Subjects upon which I am not sufficiently supplied with evidence to be convinced, yet the present bill which your Lordp. supports for the sake of the poor Worthies of another Climate, & on which your Lordp. is so well informed from your accurate investigation, induces me to request your lordp. will use my Proxy—It is a tribute I owe to humanity, may I add I dare not do otherwise as a Christian, than to contribute either at the expense of a voracious Merchant, or of a reasonable compensation for an opulent Nation, to rescue from an horrid scene of misery and destruction our own poor image of another colour....
>
> TOWNSHEND⁴⁶

⁴⁴In September 1788, Hawkesbury was voted the freedom of Liverpool for his services to that city. He replied, "Placed as I am by His Majesty at the Head of a Committee of Council appointed to have the care of the Commerce of His dominions, it is my Duty to pay the greatest Attention to the Interests of those concerned in every Branch of it, and to afford them all the Protection in my Power, on every proper Occasion...." BM Add MS 38223, 170, 175.

⁴⁵Cobbett, *Parl. Hist.*, XXXIV, 1101; and BM Add MS 38416, 143, 150.

⁴⁶*Ibid.*, 136–137, Townshend described himself as "a friend to this trade".

The question of compensation to which Lord Townshend adverted occasioned much hard feeling in the Upper House. Townshend himself favored it, as did the Duke of Richmond, the only abolitionist peer in the Cabinet, but their plea was denied by Hawkesbury on the ground of expense.[47] Not to be put off, Richmond took his case to Pitt, and in two Cabinet meetings on the 27th and 30th of June, won permission to introduce his amendment.

Compensation was originally intended to offset losses incurred under the retroactive clause of the bill. Commissioners were to be appointed by Lord Chancellor Thurlow to review and decide on the justice of the demands made by claimants. No limit was set on the amount of award and no procedure set for appeal. Such a vague outline of functions may have been common enough, but in the emotional atmosphere engendered by abolition it seemed dangerous. "What Merchant," asked Hawkesbury, "to seek his redress, can consent to be brought far from his home, & expose his Books, Accounts, & business" to the "caprice, partiality, or resentment of Commissioners?"[48] Other peers felt the same way, and compensation was passed by a margin of 14 to 12 only after Pitt made it clear that the retroactive clause of the bill could not be given up.[49]

In this as in every other debate on the bill in the Lords, Pitt and Richmond faced an almost unprecedented attack by other members of the Cabinet. Lord Sydney, "whose connection by marriage with the Chancellor of the Exchequer formed his best security for continuing in office a single day,"[50] opposed the

[47]*Ibid.*, 189. Hawkesbury calculated that compensation would amount to at least £339,700.

[48]*Ibid.*, 194. Notes for a speech.

[49]Cobbett, *Parl. Hist.*, XXVII, 651. This division has been mistakenly represented as the final passing of the complete bill, by some historians: no vote is recorded on that occasion.

[50]Henry B. Wheatley, ed., *The Historical and the Posthumous Memoirs of Sir Nathaniel Wm. Wraxall* (5 vols., London, 1884), V, 143. Hereafter cited as *Wraxall Memoirs*. Wraxall's detailed account of the progress of Dolben's bill is remarkably unbiased, and he tells why: "My admiration now follows Pitt, but I will candidly own that at the time when the events happened which are here related, I strongly inclined to embrace an opposite opinion." *Ibid.*, 146.

bill initially, then abstained out of deference to Pitt. Neither Lord Howe nor the Marquis of Carmarthen spoke, and Lord Camden did not even attend. The Duke of Chandos, who was Lord Steward, argued and voted against the bill; he possessed considerable property in Jamaica, where his wife's first husband had been Governor.[51]

The worst came from Lord Thurlow. The thick-skinned Lord Chancellor, a favorite of the King but no friend to Pitt, called the bill stupid, impracticable, and unjust. It violated the pledge of ministers to defer the matter to next session and was obviously designed to harrass the Liverpool traders. Thurlow would never accept it, even though he was to have appointed the commissioners for compensation. "Notwithstanding Pitt's personal appearance on the steps of the throne, the Chancellor, quitting the woolsack several times in the course of the debate, neither spared his invectives nor abstained from the most contemptuous expressions."[52] To the embarrassment of the House, he picked out an impetuous second-string abolitionist, Lord Stanhope, and repeatedly tore him to shreds over every clause in the bill.

The moderate reaction which Pitt showed in public toward Thurlow's outrageous behavior has been explained many times.[53] Regulation of the slave trade could not be made a Government measure because most of the Cabinet opposed it. In the 18th century ministers existed to govern and not to legislate; when Pitt insisted on legislating he was forced to do so as an individual, and could not with propriety demand the allegiance of others. Furthermore Pitt's special quality of leadership, based on acquiescence rather than on control, meant he could not insist on winning every minor issue if he wanted to retain his position.

[51]*Ibid.*, 143–144.
[52]*Ibid.*, 145. Cf. The Bishop of Bath and Wells, *The Journal and Correspondence of William, Lord Auckland* (4 vols., London, 1861), II, 221.
[53]See R. Pares, *George III and the Politicians* (Oxford, 1953), 164–165; Donald G. Barnes, *George III and William Pitt, 1783–1806* (Stanford, 1939), 175–180; and Archibald S. Foord, *His Majesty's Opposition* (Oxford, 1964) p. 414.

Privately, however, Pitt was furious. He called a Cabinet meeting for noon on June 30, and there gave his critics a final warning. He would allow Richmond to bring in a compensation clause as a concession to the trade, but if that were not accepted he would return the bill to the House of Commons immediately and make it a Cabinet issue: "if it fails then the opposers of it and myself cannot continue members of the same government."[54] He threatened, in effect, to make Thurlow responsible for thwarting a clear decision of the House of Commons, a dangerous thing for a peer to do. Pitt would then offer to resign in protest, and Thurlow's political career would be ruined. The bill was allowed to go through.

But Pitt had moved too soon. If Thurlow complied with his immediate terms, there would be no excuse to drop him from the Cabinet. Having made sure the bill would eventually pass, therefore, the Lord Chancellor resumed his attack on it. Those outside the Cabinet naturally assumed that Pitt was being ignored. Wraxall wrote later:

> So violent a contest on public grounds between two members of the same Administration in one of the Houses of Parliament, yet not followed by the resignation of either, might be considered as a sort of political paradox. I believe it has no parallel since the accession of the House of Hanover.[55]

In fact Thurlow did not resign until 1792, and the impression made by his retention, says one of Pitt's biographers, may be considered one of the causes of the failure of the abolitionists at this time.[56]

Dolben's bill, extensively altered, was given its third reading in the Lords on July 3 and sent to the lower House for ap-

---

[54] *Dropmore MSS.*, I, 342. Pitt to Grenville, June 29, 1788. Richmond's role is only hinted at in this letter, but Pitt's allusion to the Duke's compensation amendment, moved in debate only a few hours later, is clear enough.

[55] *Wraxall Memoirs*, V, 146–147.

[56] J. H. Rose, *The Life of William Pitt* (London, 1923), part I, 464–465.

proval. There Pitt found that his troubles had only begun. There were so many amendments to consider that Dolben had to incorporate them in a new bill, which was opposed at every stage by the slave trade interest. On the motion for second reading, petitions were presented from the Liverpool merchants and from Stephen Fuller on behalf of the residents of Jamaica. Both asked to be heard by counsel at the Bar of the House. Pitt again compromised. Having demonstrated that the amendments were obviously favorable to the petitioners, he induced the House to refuse hearing counsel, but he concluded by moving to give bounties for the preservation of lives in the middle passage. This suggestion was quickly incorporated, and the bill was carried up to the Lords the same day.

There, however, a mistake in framing the bill was discovered which necessitated another renewal in the lower House. The proceedings, as described by Wraxall, must have infuriated Pitt:

> The greatest difficulty consisted in procuring the number of members requisite for placing and keeping the Speaker in the chair, at a time when the session might be regarded as virtually at an end.... The enemies of Dolben's proposition might easily frustrate its success by merely counting the House, an immediate adjournment being indispensable if there were not forty members present, as soon as the circumstance became the subject of a motion. Even Treasury letters could not enforce attendance.... Sir William Dolben having moved to read his bill a second time, new petitions from Liverpool, of the same tenor with those antecedently presented, were brought up, while Mr. Gamon[57] moved to postpone the second reading for three months. On a division, thirty-five members supported the Minister.... Only two votes were found to oppose the

[57]Richard Grace Gamon (1748–1818), M. P. for Winchester, 1784–1812. He was brother-in-law to the Duke of Chandos, who brought him into Parliament, but he owned West Indian estates in his own right, probably in St. Kitt's.

measure. The four tellers completed the number to forty-one, being one more than was absolutely necessary to legalize the proceedings.[58]

Again the bill was rushed through the final stages and again it was sent to the Lords. This time, accompanied by another attack by Thurlow,[59] it passed, and on the morning of July 11, a few minutes before Parliament was prorogued, it received the royal assent.

Pitt had won, but in doing so he had compromised to an extent dangerous for the future acceptance of abolition. His most vociferous opponent remained in office beside him. Equally important, he had established the principle of compensation for commercial damages arising out of a measure relating to the slave trade. Why did he make these concessions? There is no evidence to indicate that Richmond's compensation clause made any difference to the vote of the Lords. Pitt's motion for bounties was offered to a House that divided 35-2 in his favor. There may have been, in each case, one or two crucial votes requiring special wooing; but it seems equally likely that Pitt, viewing the Regulating Bill as a test case which would determine Parliament's willingness to interfere in any way with the slave trade, simply dared take no chances. It was easy to make financial concessions because the act was to expire in one year, when the general question would supposedly be settled.[60] The bill's substance was less important than its principle.

Ironically, it was the substance that flourished for the next fifteen years. Read in the light of present standards, 28 Geo. III, c. 54 is appallingly lenient, but slave merchants at first con-

[58] *Wraxall Memoirs*, V, 148–149.
[59] Wraxall said no more discussion took place; but William Fawkener wrote to Hawkesbury July 11, "Your Lordship will probably have heard that the Lord Chancellor yesterday attacked Lord Stanhope, & almost every clause in the Bill." BM Add MS 38416, 145.
[60] Pitt himself demanded the one-year limitation to counteract the argument that regulation implied approbation of the slave trade.

sidered it ruinous and threatened to leave for France.⁶¹ 1,432 men and 8,427 tons of shipping were claimed to have been made redundant by the regulations. £4,141 were in fact granted as compensation over the next three years.⁶² During that time merchants learned to live with the bill—and to sidestep some of its provisions—while planters openly acknowledged the worth of the improvements. Dolben's act was renewed in 1789 with additional clauses to safeguard the lives and interests of seamen. Further amendments were made in 1794 and 1797, relating to insurance and the comfort of slaves. Finally, in 1799, the regulations were made permanent by 39 Geo. III, c. 80.

The circumstances in which the act was first brought forward and passed were indicative on several counts of the future course of the abolition campaign. In the first place, Pitt's parliamentary strategy had been upset by the impatience and distrust of members on the fringe of the abolition movement, who resented the interference of the Privy Council Committee for Trade. Of the three men who demanded immediate legislation, Sir William Dolben was a Pittite reformer already sixty years old who took little part in later debates, being relegated to the chairmanship of House committees on abolition. He was not informed of the circumstances which led Pitt to postpone debate in 1788. The member for Devon, John P. Bastard, generally favored the government; but he was critical, independent, and pertinacious. He had previously pressured Pitt to adopt reforms relating to transportation for criminals and to ecclesiastical courts. It was he who had demanded an immediate enquiry on the slave trade by the House. The Hon. Thomas Pelham, M. P. for Sussex, was widely respected for his generosity and concern for the welfare of others. His constituents were strongly "patriotic" and he was in opposition with Fox, who was the first to criticize the Privy Council enquiry. He himself, he said, had prepared a plan for regulation before he discovered Wilber-

---

[61]BM Add MS 38416, 152, 155: John Tarleton and James Jones to Hawkesbury.

[62]*HC Sess Pap* 1790(698)LXXXVII, 510–512; *House of Commons Journals*, February 28, 1792.

PRELUDE TO ABOLITION 51

force's intentions; but neither he nor John Bastard were active in abolitionist circles.

In the second place, all the members of both Houses who were not outright abolitionists expressed concern for the commercial interests of the nation. The slave trade, while not supporting two-thirds of the commerce of Britain (as Lord Penrhyn once claimed), was of substantial interest to a sizable section of the population around Liverpool and Manchester. Moreover, it was a trade coveted by other nations, especially the French, who were trying strenuously to take it over. As long as regulations would not damage England's competitive advantage, the moderate Members were willing to impose them. But abolition was quite another question.

Finally, the ill-informed debates on the Regulating Act of 1788 contributed greatly to the upsurge of emotional argument and dogmatic assertions which Pitt and the more responsible West Indians had hoped to avoid. On the one side, it was expected that a full and reasoned enquiry would prove that abolition was absolutely justified; on the other, that a demonstration of the interests and property involved with the trade would render its abolition unthinkable. Therein lay the double tragedy of the abolition campaign, for both assumptions were correct. And yet neither could be fully tested before they were inundated by the wave of unreasoning propaganda which now came rushing in.

4

The Case Against Abolition

The intensity of feeling displayed by James Ramsay and his persecutors was characteristic of the whole campaign for the abolition of the slave trade, both in and out of Parliament. Rational arguments were few and even the facts of the case were disputed. Liverpool merchants and West Indians, pilloried by zealous abolitionists, sometimes lost their tempers completely. William Wilberforce was threatened with violence in 1788 by a hostile witness and again in 1792 by slaving captains. In the latter year one of Wilberforce's friends accompanied him as a bodyguard on trips to his Yorkshire constituency. The correspondence of Liverpool abolitionists such as James Currie and William Roscoe had to be conducted anonymously through unsuspected associates. Dr. Currie was told as early as 1790 that his efforts were useless because Wilberforce had given up. Finally, as was to be expected, witnesses who testified to evil conditions in the colonies were ostracized by the West Indian community.[1]

Many newspapers, even those supporting Pitt's government, were anti-abolitionist. Since no parliamentary debate could be fully covered in one issue, and since verbatim reporting was

[1] *Life of Wilberforce*, I, 354–356, and II, 20.

not yet known, hostile editors could easily misrepresent arguments they disliked. The *Morning Chronicle,* for example, was usually one of the best parliamentary reporters; but Wilberforce complained about its "scandalous misreporting" of his speeches.[2]

Cartoonists found the abolition campaign a rich source of ideas. To judge from their extant work the majority were friendly to abolition. But this did not preclude an occasional poke at the crusaders' self-righteous zeal. A cartoon by Gilray, published after Wilberforce's defeat in 1796, showed him reclining on a couch, drinking West Indian rum with a fat African woman. The abolitionist Bishop Porteus held another woman on his knee, and an African servant boy attended with more rum and Havanna cigars. The caption: "Philanthropic Consolations, after the Loss of the Slave Bill."[3]

This kind of abuse formed an ugly side to the dispute, although it was never very great. Abolition, unlike many reform movements could not be combatted effectively with personal invective. The motives of its leading advocate were beyond reproach, whereas the slave traders were either unknown or notorious. A majority in Parliament already agreed that abolition in the abstract was not a bad thing. Accordingly the defenders of the slave trade set out to show that the evil consequences of the measure were far greater than its intrinsic merit. To do so they turned to the traditional methods of political persuasion, and violence gradually diminished.

The arguments for and against abolition, put forth in petitions and pamphlets, committee hearings, parliamentary debates, and private correspondence seldom changed during the next fifteen years. Wilberforce and his friends exhausted all their themes in 1789 and merely repeated them in following years. The defense, less prepared at first, gradually built up a

[2]A. Aspinall, "The Reporting and Publishing of the House of Commons Debates, 1771–1834" in Pares and Taylor, *Essays Presented to Sir Lewis Namier,* p. 249.
[3]M. Dorothy George, ed., *Catalogue of Political and Personal Satires preserved in the Department of Prints and Drawings in the British Museum,* VII (London, 1942), number 8793.

repertoire of its own. As early as 1791 the arguments for both sides were so well known that complete exposition was no longer needed. Speakers and writers could evoke whole paragraphs with a single phrase, and the entire range of opinion on abolition could be covered in a half-hour speech.

The cryptic style and the use of catchwords or insinuations are well illustrated by nineteen resolutions passed at a general meeting of West Indian planters, merchants, and other creditors on May 19, 1789.[4] By examining each one, it is possible to survey the principal arguments against the abolition of the slave trade.

(1) That slavery has always existed as a condition of mankind in Africa.

From their own experience, and from reports by European explorers, the African merchants knew that slavery was practiced by several tribes in the Niger region, and that a slave trade to the Mediterranean coast had flourished for many years. There was no evidence to contradict their assumption that such had always been the case. Therefore English merchants were justified in sharing the trade. This view was rather enlightened, compared to previous assertions that Africans were either a sub-human species or the descendants of Cain who were cursed in the Bible.[5]

(2) That slaves purchased by British Merchants were prisoners of war or convicted criminals: or they were born slaves or made so for debt.

The slave traders were accused of kidnapping or otherwise procuring innocent freemen to make up their cargoes. In answer they usually maintained that all slaves were purchased from African middlemen who certified (when asked) the servile status of the persons sold. It was not the merchants' duty to search out injustices. Furthermore, prisoners of war and crim-

[4] Minutes of the West India Planters and Merchants, cited hereafter as Min WI Plant. The resolutions were published in the morning and evening newspapers next day.
[5] For an excellent account of eighteenth-century opinion on Africa and the Africans, see Philip D. Curtin, *The Image of Africa: British Ideas and Actions, 1780–1850* (Madison, Wisconsin, 1964).

inals were put to death if not sold, so the British were doing them a favor by trading. This resolution and the following were the weakest parts of the defense, for the evidence was all on the other side. In fact a law had been passed in 1750 which prohibited the use of fraud or violence to procure slaves. Had Pitt enforced it, as he once thought of doing, he might have wrecked the African trade straight away.

(3) That the trade in slaves is the only extensive or advantageous trade possible in Africa: and that the slave trade does not necessarily tend to promote wars or retard the growth of civilization.

Abolitionists charged that the willingness of the English to buy prisoners of war encouraged the African tribes to attack each other, thus neglecting "legitimate" trade and forfeiting the benefits of European civilization (in abolitionist terminology "commerce" and "civilization" were interchangeable). On the contrary, replied merchants and West Indians together, the Africans were indolent, stupid, unproductive, and prone to blood feuds and ritual massacres. The slave trade served the cause of civilization by carrying victims of barbarism to new homes, where education, discipline, and religion were available for their benefit. In any case, it was argued, there were few products or ports on the coast of Africa for other kinds of commerce.

(4) Proprietors have a right to enjoy property legally acquired.

(5) The titles to West India property are founded on grants and sales of land by the Crown, on Royal Charters, and Acts of Parliament.

The fourth resolution was a statement of principle, the fifth a statement of fact. Both were unimpeachable, and both were designed to make abolition into a constitutional issue, centering not on the suffering Africans but on the sacrosanct property of British subjects. The whole process of turning a native into a West Indian agricultural laborer—the methods of trade, the Atlantic passage, the seasoning—was ignored. But the idea of property, the most important and successful of all West Indian arguments, was further developed in the next six resolutions.

(6) That the capital now vested in the sugar colonies, in land, Negroes, buildings, live and dead stock, amounts to seventy millions of Pounds Sterling.

The figure of £70 million was based on a rather loose estimate made by the Society of Planters and Merchants in a letter to Lord Hawkesbury. It exceeded the more "official" evaluation of a clerk of the Privy Council by £6 million. But the West Indians could and did cite "The Privy Council Report" in their speeches, because Hawkesbury included both estimates.[6] Either one was well calculated to impress the public with the enormity of the risk involved in abolishing the supply of labor which secured such an investment. Even £64 million was over three times the annual national budget for Britain.[7] Moreover, high feeling stirred up by abolition tended to force this calculated risk out of the range of eventual probability into that of immediate certainty. "Abolition will knock out seventy millions of property at one blow" became the standard phrase in West Indian perorations. A tribute to the effectiveness of this argument was paid by George Canning in 1802, when he directed a speech to "those gentlemen unconnected with the West Indies themselves, who had yet always made West Indian interests the plea and pretence for their votes in favor of the slave trade".[8]

(7) The value of the West Indies depends solely on cultivation, and will be depreciated by any system depriving the proprietors of the means of cultivation.

(8) The use of Negroes has been the universal practice from the infancy of the colonies in all the islands, British or foreign.

(9) The constitutions of Europeans are unequal to agricultural labour in the West Indies.

[6] *PC Rpt 1789*, part IV, nos. 17 and 18.
[7] J. Steven Watson, *The Reign of George III* (Oxford, 1960), 292, puts the total revenue for 1786 at £18½ million, that for 1792 at a million more.
[8] Cobbett, *Parl. Hist.*, XXXVI, 866.

The conclusion intended, of course, was that the value of the West Indies was based on the use of Negro laborers. No mention was made of machines, which the planters contended (not very convincingly) were used wherever possible. The belief that white laborers could not stand the climate was historically invalid. Barbados and other early colonies were first cultivated by white indentured servants and exiled criminals. Negro labor was introduced only because it was cheaper and more plentiful.[9] The continuing need to purchase more Negroes showed that they were no more equal than Europeans to the demands of West Indian agriculture. The proprietors were really saying that Negro lives were more expendable than others.

The wording of resolutions 7, 8, and 9 is significant. They discuss "means of cultivation," "Negroes," and "agricultural labour", but not "slavery". One is tempted to dismiss this as simple subterfuge, but after reading the whole of the abolition debates, as well as the minutes of the West Indian bodies and the correspondence of their members, one is inclined to believe that the planters actually did not think of their Negroes as slaves in the classical sense. The abolitionists did, because they were absorbed in the wrongs of Africa and held rather categorical views about the injustice of exchanging men for money. But their cult of the "noble savage", derived from ideas of natural reason engendered by the French Enlightenment, was totally incomprehensible to the resident West Indians. Having paid good money for their laborers, the planters were obliged to train them during three years of seasoning, provide them with food, clothing, houses, and private gardens, and then exercise a constant vigil over their activities. The anarchic social regime fostered by negligence and the inequality of the sexes produced generally irresponsible laborers who, as they gained experience in the routine of the estate, became adept at sabotaging production schedules. Threats, pleas, and bribes were often necessary to get the work done on schedule. In these circumstances, the planters' cynical attitude toward their op-

[9] Eric Williams, *Capitalism and Slavery* (Chapel Hill, N. C., 1944), 19-20.

ponents' abstract notions of injustice is easily understood if not excused.

Residents of the islands were careful to dissociate themselves from the slave merchants, as they had some right to do. A committee of the Jamaica House of Assembly, in a report of October 1788 to the Privy Council Committee for Trade, approved the new Slave Trade Regulating Act and made suggestions for further improvements in trading conditions. However, the committee added,

> It seems not to be understood in Great Britain, that the Inhabitants of the West India Islands have no Concern in the Ships trading to Africa. The African Trade is purely a British Trade, carried on by British Subjects residing in Great Britain on Capitals of their own. The Connection and Intercourse between the Planters of these islands, and the Merchants of Great Britain trading to Africa, extend no further than the mere Purchase of what British Acts of Parliament have declared to be legal objects of Purchase.[10]

On the other hand, as the next resolutions pointed out, the "mere purchase" of slaves was vital to the existence of the islands.

(10) Natural causes and accidental calamities make a constant, and at times rapid decrease in the number of Negroes, which cannot be guarded against or provided for by births.

There were two arguments here. The first, that population decline due to natural causes was greater than the birth rate, was directly challenged by Wilberforce and became the central issue in the parliamentary campaign for abolition. A significant proportion of slave mortality, said Wilberforce, was caused not by nature at all but by cruel treatment. Abolitionists vied with each other for the most horrible tales of whipping, mutilation,

[10] *PC Rpt 1789*, part III, appendix, "Jamaica".

THE CASE AGAINST ABOLITION

murder, and sexual outrage, recounted in the pseudo-solemn manner of the modern tabloid newspaper. These crimes, it was charged, were due directly to the slave trade, for planters would not think of maltreating their slaves if they could not easily and cheaply be replaced. The Negro population would grow of its own accord if the trade were prohibited.

If Dolben's recital of horrors in 1788 is representative, such attacks made a substantial impression on the House of Commons. A single story, even if baseless or badly distorted, was sufficient to hold the public's interest. The image was sharp, the feelings easily aroused, the moral clear and simple. West Indians could reply that the incidents were not indicative of general conditions (which they said were better than those enjoyed by most European peasants) but support of the status quo was of course a weak and uninteresting defense.[11]

Planters also argued that they had done everything in their power to increase the slave population by natural means. It was shown in Chapter I that this was probably not true. Many of the absentee planters who told the House of Commons that breeding was impossible admitted under cross-examination that they had no knowledge of births and deaths on their own plantations. The exception was Sir Ralph Payne,[12] one of whose estates in Antigua had increased its population steadily for many years. Sir Ralph explained that he knew nothing about planting; his Negroes just happened to be all Christianized creoles who preferred to marry among themselves and devote their time to family life on the plantation, rather than mix with

[11]One "fact" circulated by abolitionists, and widely repeated then and since, is that one-third of the imported Negroes died from "seasoning" in three years. The story was started by James Ramsay, who misread a passage of Edward Long's *History of Jamaica* (II, 434) dealing with mortality due to yaws contracted during the Atlantic passage. But Sheridan ("Organization of the Slave Trade") quotes several West Indians to the effect that at least one quarter of all new slaves did die during the period of seasoning.

[12]Sir Ralph Payne, 1st baronet, created Baron Lavington (Ireland) in 1795, Governor of the Leeward Islands, 1771-5 and 1799-1807. M. P. (various constituencies) in 1768-1771, 1776-1784, 1795-1799. Described as a pompous, vain man with a sonorous voice, a rich socialite.

"lower class" African neighbors. This arrangement was made easier by the large proportion of female slaves resident on the estate.[13]

It should have been obvious that conditions like those on Sir Ralph's estate were essential for raising the birth rate, but neither planters nor abolitionists seem to have seen this at the time. Wilberforce, having never been near the West Indies, concentrated on stories of cruelty which had more propaganda value. He never took the trouble to talk to the West Indians themselves about possible improvements. However, even Sir Ralph considered his estate to be a purely fortuitous exception.

The second argument in resolution (10) concerned the recurrence of epidemics and climatic disasters. As already noted, thousands of slaves were lost when drought, disease, or hurricanes swept through the islands. Planters maintained that no amount of breeding could protect them against the sudden demise of ten or twenty per cent of their labor force for the plantations would fall to ruins before a new generation grew up. Consequently some imports of slaves had to be allowed, whether the general trade was abolished or not. To this argument the abolitionists made no reply. For them it was only one more minor inconvenience to be weighed against the infinite injustice of the slave trade itself.

The dispute over breeding went sadly astray because neither side possessed adequate information. The island legislatures, in their reports to Lord Hawkesbury in 1788–1789, showed the same ignorance of slave births and deaths as the absentee planters mentioned above. When a census of slaves was finally taken it was found that the whole argument had been pointless. By 1830 the creole population was increasing at the rate of 1–2% per year whereas slaves born in Africa still died much faster than they could reproduce.[14] Furthermore, in all the colonies except Trinidad, Demerara, and Berbice (which still had a

[13]*HC Sess Pap* 1790(698)LXXXVII, 439. Sir Ralph's grandfather had used this estate as a breeding ground, over-stocking it with female slaves.
[14]*HC Sess Pap* 1831–2(381)XX, 318–319. Edward Long made a similar observation in the 1774 edition of his *History of Jamaica.* II (book iii, chapter 3), 432.

great proportion of African-born slaves), female slaves now outnumbered males, an exact reversal of pre-abolition conditions. It must be concluded that the slave population as a whole had been declining, and would continue to decline until most of the Africans had died.

Wilberforce was therefore correct in assuming that a successful policy of breeding slaves was dependent upon the abolition of the trade from Africa. But he failed to see that change of environment, not cruelty, was the main cause of the problem. Africans no less than Europeans were susceptible to being transported thousands of miles to work in the West Indian climate. On the other hand, planters were equally correct in predicting economic decline in the British colonies if abolition were passed. The number of workers available for agricultural production was bound to decrease for at least a generation, until African deaths were compensated by creole births. The loss thus incurred could not be made up for half a century or more.

(11) That to depend solely on the internal Negroe population for cultivation, is to rest the interests not only of the planters but also of mortgagees, annuitants, femmes couverts, widows, infants, and various other West India creditors, in Great Britain, on the uncertain issue of an untried speculative experiment, which, if it fails in the ends proposed, must cause great loss if not total ruin, to numbers of innocent individuals, who are purchasers, for a valuable consideration, on the faith of a system long established on the colonies, sanctioned and corroborated by many Acts of Parliament.

This resolution resumed the catalogue of interests involved with the slave trade, linking it with the constitutional question of property rights. Acts of Parliament which encouraged the slave trade, the West Indian economy, loans to planters, or colonies in general were cited to prove that the slave system was sanctioned by traditional British law. George Hibbert in 1790 listed thirty such precedents.[15] Edward Law (later Lord Ellen-

---

[15] *HC Sess Pap* 1790(698)LXXXVII, 390–391.

borough, Addington's ally) in a speech to the House of Lords two years later, gave twenty-seven.[16] It was argued that the probable damaging consequences of abolition would deprive plantation owners and creditors of the value of their investments without benefit of trial. Moreover, the measure penalized a particular section of the British public and was therefore basically unconstitutional. These arguments were strong enough to turn every lawyer in the House against Wilberforce.[17]

(12) The trade to Africa and the British West Indies supports manufactures, shipbuilding, navigation, and revenues; and depends on the continuing cultivation of the West Indies.

(13) [A list of exports to Africa and the West Indies, by value, quoted from the Privy Council Committee Report of 1789.]

(14) [The value of imports from the West Indies, the tonnage of ships in the West India and Africa trades, the number of seamen employed, and the revenue derived from commercial tariffs.]

The figures changed from year to year: in 1790, exports to Africa were valued at £929,203, in 1793 at £384,587, and in 1799 at £1,626,624.[18] But the argument was always the same. Too much money and too many people were involved with the slave-based commerce of Africa and the West Indies to risk total destruction by an untried, speculative experiment like abolition.

(15) That the West India and African trades constitute a nursery for seamen.

This was the most frequently used, and soon the most nauseating, of the defensive slogans. The loss of seamen on board West

[16]BM Add MS 12433, 15. A clause in Royal Grants of land in the islands ceded by France in 1763, ordering one-half the uncultivated land to be cleared within ten years of purchase, was often used to buttress this argument. The last grant, however, had been made in 1774. *HC Sess Pap* 1790(698)LXXXVII, 221–223.

[17]*Life of Wilberforce*, I, 293.

[18]Sir Frederick Morton Eden, *Eight Letters on the Peace, and on the Commerce and Manufactures of Great Britain and Ireland.* (London, 2nd ed., 1802), 110, from custom house accounts.

Indian ships was about 1.5% of original crews, a respectable record. But on slaving ships the average loss was as high as 21.5%.[19] Abolitionists rightly called Africa the grave, not the nursery, of seamen. Most perished from disease or the effects of climate, but many others died or deserted because of wretched working conditions and inhuman treatment by ships' captains.[20] The seamen "nursed" in overseas commerce were valued chiefly as recruits for the British Navy. But slaving crews arriving in the West Indies were found to be too sick or too depraved for even the most wretched forms of service. Sailors were often thrown off the slave ship, sick and without pay, after the captain had picked a quarrel for the purpose. Then they were left to rot in the West Indies, while the slave ship returned to England with a skeleton crew to save costs.[21]

African merchants replied that the trade was still a nursery for seamen because one-fourth to one-half the crews were former landlubbers, who received their first naval training on a slave ship. This argument was also disproved by reference to the facts.[22] In general, the various Slave Trade Regulating Acts from 1788 to 1799, with their clauses for improving the treatment of crews, showed that Parliament was never deceived about the "nursery for seamen."

(16) That the French give bounties on shipping and importing African labourers.

(17) That the Spanish recently opened several ports in South America for the importation of Negroes, duty free, for the encouragement of agriculture in their colonies.

(18) That the Americans have fitted out several vessels to prosecute this trade.

[19]*HC Sess Pap* 1790-1(745-748)XXXIV, 281. The figures were compiled by Thomas Clarkson, at the risk of his life, from ships' muster rolls in Bristol and Liverpool. They were checked and found accurate by Pitt and Hawkesbury. Cf. BM Add MS 38416, 180.
[20]*PC Rpt 1789*, part I: sixty pages of evidence produced by Clarkson and his witnesses.
[21]*Ibid.*; and Governor Parry of Barbadoes to Lord Sydney, CO 28:61, 1770.
[22]Cobbett, *Parl. Hist.*, XXIX, 322.

The threat of foreign competition was the second most important argument against abolition. It was pointed out, quite correctly, that the trade abandoned by the British would only be transferred to French, Spanish, American, and other foreign merchants, with a consequent loss of revenue and navigation for Britain. And there would be no real relief for the Africans.[23] In fact, since the passing of the Regulating Act of 1788, British slave ships were cleaner and relatively more comfortable than those of foreign traders, so that a unilateral abolition would actually make conditions worse.

Wilberforce hoped to persuade the other European nations to give up the trade along with Britain, but his efforts were in vain. Sir James Harris reported from Holland as early as May 1788 that unless there were a general European agreement, Dutch slave traders would not budge.[24] Spanish dealers arrived in Liverpool in February 1788 looking for information on African goods and ships[25] and exactly one year later the Spanish king cancelled all his British slaving contracts in order to promote a national trade. All but a few designated ports in the Spanish colonies were then closed to foreign imports of slaves. High taxes and business restrictions were imposed on outsiders, while Spanish traders received bounties.[26]

The shipowners of Bristol, in a petition of May 12, 1789, reported that "since the Restrictions lately laid on the Trade to Africa by the British Legislature, no less than Forty Sail of Vessels have been fitted out for that Coast in the States of New England."[27] The number may have been exaggerated, but Pitt was impressed enough to prepare a bill against such ships fitting out in British ports to save money.[28]

[23]Cf. Rose, *Life of Pitt,* part I, 467; also Romilly's report to Madame Dumont in *The Memoirs of Sir Samuel Romilly* (London, 1840), book I, 343.
[24]*Dropmore MSS,* III, 442–443. Cf. *PC Rpt 1789,* part IV, Declaration of the States of Holland, May 11, 1788.
[25]BM Add Ms 38416, 26–30. William Walton of Liverpool to Hawkesbury.
[26]*PC Rpt 1789,* part VI, "Spain"; *HC Sess Pap* 1790(698)LXXXVII, 190–191, testimony of J. Baillie.
[27]*House of Commons Journals,* May 12, 1789.
[28]*Dropmore MSS,* II, 105, Pitt to Grenville.

THE CASE AGAINST ABOLITION   65

Fear of the French was the greatest obstacle to abolition among many members of Parliament. British naval officers reported that the African trade was a vital source of French naval power, and that in response to the recently introduced bounties on tonnage the number and size of French slaving ships had increased rapidly. These facts kept several friends, in spite of their liberal sentiments, from voting for Wilberforce.[29] William Eden, the ambassador in Paris, reported a definite hostility to abolition among French officials and held out little hope for a change.[30] Indeed, English slave traders were being invited by the French government to sail under French colors to St. Domingue.[31] It was clear that so long as the French were capable of sailing to Africa and the West Indies, a unilateral abolition by Britain would have little effect on the number of Negroes carried into slavery.

(19) That the prime minister's declaration, that no compensation could be paid for abolition, is so repugnant to every principle of justice that it will destroy all faith in Royal Charters and in Parliament.

In accordance with the traditions of British law, which usually compensated those materially injured by acts of state, the slave traders argued that provision must be made in the abolition bill itself for covering the loss of their legitimate commerce. West Indian planters supported this argument, adding their own claims for damage, predicated on the supposed decline of their agricultural labor supply. They solemnly assured the British public that the success of Wilberforce's bill would mean greatly increased taxes, or that the amount of compensation necessary was so great as to make abolition impossible. When Pitt declared that no compensation should be paid for the prohibition of crime,[32] he violated the precedent set by his own

[29]*Life of Wilberforce*, I, 226. Also R. and S. Wilberforce, eds., *The Correspondence of William Wilberforce*, (London, 1840), I, 167.
[30]Rose, *Life of Pitt*, part I, 459; *Life of Wilberforce*, I, 155–158.
[31]*House of Lords Journals*, July 3, 1788, letters from John Tarleton.
[32]Cobbett, *Parl. Hist.*, XXVIII, 78.

Slave Trade Regulating Act. West Indian colonists threatened to declare independence or to remove to some foreign territory with all their goods and slaves, if such injustice was carried out. All these nineteen resolutions may be classified as arguments for the protection of either property or commerce. Yet clearly not only private interests were involved. The whole nation had a stake in the African and West Indian trades, and the trustees of the nation's revenue and navigation who sat at Westminster could not be expected to forget it.

While early historians rightly dramatized the abolition question as a clash between morality and material interest, they were mistaken in assigning these motives to separate persons. Many, if not most, members of Parliament agreed with both sides. It was a painful dilemma, one that split families even in Liverpool.[33] Time did not always solve the problem. Lord Eldon, who had always opposed Wilberforce, wrote to him about 1804, "I wish my mind had been so framed as to feel no doubts on this awful and fearful business."[34] The problem remained a lack of information about mortality, about labor efficiency, about ships and about French commerce. The "untried speculative experiment" demanded a sacrifice no one could calculate, for a purpose no one could deny.

The arguments put forward by the Society of Planters and Merchants in May 1789 remained effective for at least thirteen years. They did not, however, include a type of criticism which was, according to many observers, the primary reason for the failure of abolition between 1792 and 1801. This criticism was based on the abolitionists' association with events in France and French West Indies. A brief discussion will show how the arguments developed; their effectiveness will be measured in the next two chapters.

Soon after the outbreak of revolution in 1789, French-African mulattoes living in Paris incited their fellows in the Caribbean island of St. Domingue to proclaim, by force of

[33]Currie, *Memoirs*, I, 135–136.
[34]A. M. Wilberforce, ed., *The Private Papers of William Wilberforce* (London, 1897), 122.

arms, the new principles of equality and fraternity. Several rebellions took place during the next year and a half, all without success. But in May 1791, certain classes of St. Domingue mulattoes, left unfranchised by a recent decree of the convention, allied themselves with thousands of Negro slaves to start a general massacre of white citizens. In September the Convention revoked the whole doctrine of mulatto equality, ruining every chance for reconciliation.

The government in Paris, determined to retain St. Domingue at all costs, refrained initially from testing the allegiance of the white settlers with permanent laws against racial discrimination. But as the uprisings became more widespread and more successful, a decision was made to support the mulattoes' demands. A decree of equality for all free men was issued in April 1792. Government commissioners with troops were sent out in September. When the whites resisted, slaves were incited to revolt and join the troops. St. Domingue rushed into chaos.

News of the first rebellions reached London in November 1791 and caused an uproar in the West Indian community. St. Domingue, with its large estates and absentee landlords, was very similar to the British islands. It was almost within shooting distance of Jamaica as well. Frightened British planters lost no time in laying the disaster at the feet of Wilberforce. The slaves of St. Domingue, they cried, were not killing to escape a detestable tyranny but were goaded on by the fanatic and ruthless abolitionists of France and England, who rejoiced in the destruction of the colonists.[35]

The Society of Planters and Merchants took up the cry in business and government circles and almost succeeded in wrecking Wilberforce's legislative program. The abolitionist leader wrote:

> People here are all panic-struck with the transaction in St. Domingo, and the apprehension or pretended apprehension of the like in Jamaica and other of our islands.

[35] Cobbett, *Parl. Hist.*, XXIX, 1075.

I am pressed on all hands... to defer my motion to next year.[36]

Even Pitt was reluctant to go ahead against public opinion. The King, who had previously tolerated Wilberforce's crusade, now opposed the whole idea.[37]

Through their implied responsibility for the atrocities in St. Domingue, and through their association with the Société des Amis des Noirs in Paris, the British abolitionists were linked to the principles and to the increasingly ugly developments of the French Revolution. "What does the abolition of the slave trade mean more or less in effect," exclaimed the Earl of Abingdon, "than liberty and equality? What more or less than the rights of man? And what is liberty and equality; and what are the rights of man, but the foolish fundamental principles of this new philosophy?"[38]

Wilberforce could not protect his followers from this onslaught. Too many of them were involved with radical reform societies, such as the Association of the Friends of the People, which had flirted with French ideas and were now victims of reaction. "It is certainly true, and perfectly natural," he wrote, "that these Jacobins are all friendly to the abolition; and it is no less true and natural that this operates to the injury of our cause."[39] Wilberforce himself had corresponded with Brissot, Siéyes and Robespierre when helping them to organize the Société des Amis des Noirs in 1787-88. Now his right-hand man, Thomas Clarkson, had declared himself a friend to the Revolution and was drawing the fire of powerful men like Henry Dundas.[40] Even the methods of abolitionist agitation—the petitions, the sermons, the great county meetings—were being attacked as seditious.

In these circumstances West Indians and slave traders had

[36] *Life of Wilberforce*, I, 340.
[37] W. E. H. Lecky, quoted in Frank J. Klingberg, *The Anti-Slavery Movement in England* (New Haven, 1926), 94.
[38] Cobbett, *Parl. Hist.*, XXX, 654.
[39] *Life of Wilberforce*, I, 343.
[40] *Ibid.*, 344.

only to repeat the popular slogans. Despite an Achilles' heel of their own,[41] they generally adopted a posture of staunch patriotism, in which the defense of the realm was fused with the defense of the slave trade.

It is difficult to measure the effect of the arguments derived from events in France and St. Domingue. Most West Indians, and some abolitionists, thought them sufficient to sway the House, but there is no evidence to prove it. The recorded debates show that no moderate or disinterested member of Parliament ever justified a vote against abolition by reference to either revolution, whereas both property and commerce were frequently used for that purpose. Moreover, although the rise of a Negro republic in St. Domingue continued to threaten the British planters, the spread of French revolutionary ideas was checked by Napoleon. After 1801 the abolitionists were relatively safe from the charge of sedition. Yet they did not triumph for another six years.

Because abolition has usually been viewed as a moral question, its historians have overlooked difficulties in politics and parliamentary procedure which might have affected its progress. The available evidence suggests that such difficulties were especially important just when anti-revolutionary feeling is claimed to have been most obstructive to measures of reform.

[41]Banastre Tarleton, friend of Fox, helped lead the fight against war with France in 1793. He was branded a Jacobin by his own brother, John, in the election of 1796.

5

The Parliamentary Conflict, 1789-1792

The rules of parliamentary procedure, which had bedeviled Dolben's regulating bill of 1788, were manipulated in subsequent sessions with increasing skill by those who defended the slave trade. Divisions were delayed or hurried forward, more evidence was demanded, and overexcited abolitionists were called to order for their remarks. Delay was the object in most cases, although sometimes there were reasonable grounds for delay.

Of course no motion for postponement of debate or for the hearing of further evidence could pass without the consent of a majority of members present. When attendance in the House was small, the West Indians themselves might make a majority. But until 1793 such opportunities were not frequent, and the West Indian community lacked the organization to take advantage of them. They chiefly had to rely on the votes of sympathizers. Divisions in the sessions from 1789 to 1792, therefore, may be taken as expressions of Parliament's general attitude toward abolition, and toward the tactics of its advocates.

One of the important arguments for abolition to emerge from the debates of 1788, which was strengthened by testimony before the Privy Council Committee for Trade, was that West

THE PARLIAMENTARY CONFLICT, 1789-1792   71

Indian slaves had no legal protection against excessive punishment, poor diet, or overwork.[1] The planters might deny specific stories of cruelty but they could not erase the general impression of tyranny created by their existing legislation. The British public would not accept assurances that the antiquated slave codes were tempered in practice by local customs and by the paternal instincts of individual planters. The fact that the penalty for killing a slave was less than that for stealing a loaf of bread in England led to the assumption that the former offense was as common as the latter. To improve their image, both Jamaica and Grenada passed revised codes of law in 1788. The Jamaicans had done the same thing four years earlier, but older regulations had not been repealed. Now, as the Slave Trade Regulating Bill entered Parliament, the Jamaica Assembly wiped the slate clean and issued a consolidated slave code, which did not alter the status of the Negroes in the slightest degree, but which was mildly worded and liberal in appearance. The Jamaican agent in London, Stephen Fuller, printed up about 700 copies of the code, "for the use of both Houses of Parliament, and the satisfaction of the Public at Large."[2]

Agent Fuller and the Jamaica legislature continued their defense before the Privy Council Committee on abolition. In answer to Lord Hawkesbury's questionnaire they put forth many assertions later quoted in Parliament (for example, "the work of the negro slave in Jamaica is far less than that of a labourer in Britain"). Fuller also brought in five or six high-ranking naval officers, who had served in the Caribbean, to support his claims.[3]

The Privy Council Committee finished its work in March, 1789. Witnesses of every description had been examined and all

[1] *PC Rpt 1789*, part III, "Barbadoes," testimony of Governor Parry and agent John Brathwaite.
[2] BM Add MS 38416, 129. The printed code may be found in *HC Sess Pap* 1789(634)XXIX; another copy, with MS notes by Edward Long, is in BM Add MS 12432, 42.
[3] BT 3:1, 260; and *PC Rpt 1789*, part III, "Further evidence on treatment of slaves in the West Indies."

but a few of Hawkesbury's questionnaires had been returned.[4] Hawkesbury probably wished to continue the enquiry until every scrap of evidence was in, but Pitt was anxious to bring the issue of abolition before the House of Commons. Now that both Wilberforce and George III had recovered from dangerous illnesses,[5] serious debate could begin.

On April 9, 1789 warnings of Wilberforce's impending motion were sent by the London West Indian associations to manufacturers and merchants in all the larger trading towns throughout Great Britain. Delegates and witnesses were asked to attend the House of Commons. Sugar factors began pressing fellow London merchants for support, while planters raised the "trade" levy on their produce from one penny to sixpence to pay for lawyers and pamphlets.[6] At Bristol a subcommittee of the Merchant Venturer's Society, authorized "to go hand in hand with the Gentlemen of London", drew up six different petitions.[7] Liverpool representatives came back to the capital for another round of testimony. They were anxious but not frightened, for this time they had allies.

The abolitionists led off with an unusual strategem, based on the Privy Council Committee report. Pitt wrote to Wilberforce on April 10:

> Grenville and I have formed a prospect of reducing the case, as it appears from the Report, into a string of resolutions, which we will send you as soon as they are complete. Our idea is, that by bringing into one view all the leading points of the case, we shall bring on the discussion

[4]Hawkesbury noted in a preface to the *PC Rpt 1789* that reports from several foreign countries were still missing.
[5]George III's temporary insanity, which ended in March 1789, precluded any debate which might have led to legislation needing his signature. It will be recalled that Wilberforce was so ill in 1788 that his resolution was presented to the House of Commons by Pitt.
[6]Min WI Plant, April 9 and April 24, 1789.
[7]Bristol University, Pinney Papers, letter book 8, 208: John Pinney to James Tobin, April 13, 1789.

to great advantage, and insure making a strong impression on the public. Many of them would be such as the opposers could hardly controvert, and would serve as the best foundation for the general motion, either for a bill or an address.[8]

Pitt apparently hoped to carry the abolition campaign, with all its enthusiasm, right onto the floor of the House. All but one of his twelve resolutions[9] were actually statements of "fact" critical of the slave trade, which members of Parliament were supposed to sanction, almost as an act of faith, in the face of contrary evidence from equally respectable sources. The whole idea was incredibly naïve. In effect, Pitt was asking members whose opinions were known to be confused and divided to agree publicly to identical reasons for abolition, even before the measure itself was considered.

Immediately after Wilberforce introduced the resolutions to the House on May 12, Lord Penrhyn and Bamber Gascoyne controverted his facts, figures, and quotations, charging that "no reliance whatsoever could be placed on the picture he had chosen to exhibit."[10] Both Burke and Fox, while offering general support, judged Pitt's resolutions unnecessary and timewasting. Even Pitt himself, sensing the mood of the House, grew doubtful.[11]

In a short time the defense had wrecked what was left of the carefully prepared case against the slave trade. What would happen to investors in West Indian property, they asked. Why was Wilberforce so intent on defaming the West Indian pro-

[8] *Life of Wilberforce*, I, 215.
[9] The resolutions are printed in *HC Sess Pap* 1789(626)LXXXII. They do not mention French rivalry in the slave trade. Pitt and his friends hoped Necker, recalled to power in October 1788, would be favorable to their cause; but his reply to their enquiry was so discouraging that they kept it secret (Romilly, *Memoirs*, I, 343). Wilberforce continued to hold out hope of French cooperation with the British in abolition.
[10] Cobbett, *Parl. Hist.*, XXVIII, 67.
[11] *Ibid.*, 72.

prietors? What about compensation, navigation, regulation, emancipation, and previous legislation? Finally, why should the House give up its historic right to take its own evidence and submit to the dictates of Lord Hawkesbury and the Privy Council?

This last objection had the support of many neutral members. They and the pro-slave trade group refused to go into committee on the resolutions unless witnesses were summoned to explain the other side of the question.[12] Wilberforce reluctantly agreed. The House sat through nine days of testimony, ending on June 23, and then London's Alderman Newnham moved to discharge the committee until the following session. No more was heard of the twelve resolutions.[13]

Abolitionists then and since have charged that the West Indian representatives used delaying tactics because they had no honest defense. Such was not the case. West Indians were primarily concerned to present their side of the question to the House in person because the majority of members, not having read the voluminous report of the Privy Council Committee, would otherwise make a decision on the basis of superior abolitionist propaganda. Given a fair hearing, West Indians were anxious to settle as quickly as possible a question which disturbed their personal and financial security. Thus when Wilberforce asked, in January 1790, for a select committee to expedite the hearing of evidence, Sir William Young readily agreed.[14] Those London and Liverpool slave traders, who really did want delay, were again isolated.

The select committee appointed in 1790 continued to hear witnesses against abolition. After the Liverpool delegates had finished, West Indian planters and merchants were called in.

---

[12] The petitions necessary to authorize an enquiry on its behalf were sent in by the London Society of Planters and Merchants on May 19.
[13] Ragatz, *Fall of the Planter Class*, 252, says they were passed without a division, but I can find no evidence of it. The resolutions did go into a committee of the House, but were never reported out.
[14] Cobbett, *Parl. Hist.*, XXVIII, 313.

Some of them tried to give an impression of neutrality,[15] but almost all were members of the London or Bristol West Indian societies, whose testimony was carefully prepared by a special body of fifteen sugar merchants.[16] Two members of the select committee themselves spoke for the defense.

This procedure was not an attempt to subvert justice. In the case of a private member's bill, a committee's sole duty was to examine any witness supplied by the petitioners and to report a faithful precis of the evidence, no matter how absurd, to the House. It could not express an opinion of any kind.[17]

The select committee made its last report of the evidence against abolition on April 1, 1790. Soon after, the West India Planters and Merchants announced in the newspapers that the evidence was "so full, impartial, and satisfactory" that they would waive the right of summing up by counsel before the House.[18] Lord Penrhyn, Chairman of the Society, was asked to accelerate a decision as much as possible.

It appears from what happened next that Wilberforce had continued examining his own witnesses before the committee of the whole House, while the Select Committee was hearing the opposition. His was always the last business of the day, few Members attended, and little progress was made. Only a few abolitionist witnesses had spoken by April 23, when Bamber Gascoyne asked for a call of the House in three weeks' time to take a final vote on the whole question. The impracticability and ruinous consequences of abolition had already been proved, he claimed. Further evidence was unnecessary. Every moment that Wilberforce spent in hearings increased the danger of Negro revolts.

[15] James Tobin, who acted as a liaison between the West Indian groups in Bristol and London, deliberately refrained from signing any petition, so that he would appear unbiased as a witness. Cf. Pinney Papers, letter book 8, 220. For Tobin's testimony see *HC Sess Pap* 1790(698)LXXXVII, 283–4.
[16] Min WI Plant, February 11, 1790.
[17] Williams, *Private Bill Procedure*, I, 31.
[18] Min WI Plant, April 25, 1790.

Wilberforce was understandably infuriated by this hypocritical subterfuge, and the House as a whole was not flattered. Instead, it re-appointed the select committee to take the remaining evidence in favor of abolition.[19]

During the next two sessions Wilberforce had difficulty finding witnesses familiar with the slave trade who were also of acceptable character. After many voyages to Africa seamen tended to look and act depraved, and there were several antagonists on the select committee eager to expose the unreliability of abolitionist evidence.[20] Witnesses who told stories of cruelty perpetrated by planters (or their wives) were often revealed as mere gossip-mongers by West Indian M. P.'s who had full details of the alleged incidents from their correspondents in the colonies.

By carefully cross-examining each witness, the defenders of the slave trade were able to extend the proceedings into the following session. But on February 4, 1791, when Wilberforce asked for re-appointment of the select committee, he was criticized[21] for delaying a decision and thereby causing "great mischief" to planters and merchants. The West Indian members withdrew from the committee to dramatize their impatience, while Banastre Tarleton, newly elected for Liverpool, gave notice that he would move the question of abolition in six weeks, committee or no.[22]

Wilberforce took advantage of the warning to bring on his star witnesses, who drew such a gruesome picture of slave conditions that the House was openly shocked.[23] This evidence was laid on the table of the House just before Tarleton was to have

[19] A comparison of the *House of Commons Journals* for January 27 and April 23, 1790, will show the identity of the two select committees. The earlier testimony is in *HC Sess Pap* 1790(698)LXXXVII; that taken after April 23 is in *HC Sess Pap* 1790(699)LXXXVIII, continued the following session in 1790–1(745)XCII.

[20] *Life of Wilberforce*, I, 261–262, 279.

[21] By J. Fenton Cawthorne, the new M. P. for Lincoln, a member of the Society of Planters and Merchants.

[22] Cobbett, *Parl. Hist.*, XXVIII, 1207–1208.

[23] Cf. *HC Sess Pap* 1790–1(748)XXXIV. The tales of slave ship surgeons were particularly nauseating.

made his motion. The West Indian societies, realizing the consequences, authorized Sir William Young and Samuel Long to block discussion by moving the previous question, if Tarleton persisted in trying to speak.[24] At a meeting on March 18 Young, Tarleton, and Wilberforce agreed to postpone the debate for another three weeks.[25]

By the time Wilberforce was finally able to launch his attack the effect created by his recent witnesses had begun to wear off, while other events had come to the fore. On March 15 news arrived of an attempted revolt by slaves in Dominica. The Society of Planters and Merchants immediately asked Lord Grenville for military protection, and on April 5 sent him a memorial (which was also printed for public circulation) blaming the incident on his abolitionist friends.[26]

Wilberforce had thus lost his advantage when he rose in the House on April 18 to plead again for abolition. He had decided, he said, to bring in a general motion for abolition, using his former propositions only as a guide for discussion. He then moved into another impassioned oration, trying to show that the slave trade was ruinous to all concerned and that while living in England the absentee planters, however liberal their sentiments, could not improve the lot of the slaves. It was a splendid performance, but Wilberforce knew he was lost. At the end of his speech he affected indifference to the present decision of the House. "Let us not despair; it is a blessed cause, and success, ere long, will crown our exertions."[27]

Tarleton rose to reply with a speech which for sheer stubbornness could not be beat. Despite the mountain of evidence lying on the table, he pledged his word as a gentleman that the slave trade was a nursery for seamen. "He could distinctly state" that Liverpool ships never lost above one per cent of their crews in the Atlantic passage. Abolition, he said, would "instantly annihilate" an export trade worth £800,000 annually,

[24] Min WI Plant, March 18, 1791.
[25] *Life of Wilberforce*, II, 288.
[26] Min WI Plant, April 5, 1791.
[27] Cobbett, *Parl. Hist.*, XXIX, 250–278.

gradually destroy the West Indies, and ruin the British navy.[28]

Tarleton's inanities were seconded by the West Indians. Thomas Grosvenor, for instance, acknowledged "it was not an amiable trade, but neither was the trade of a butcher an amiable trade, and yet a mutton chop was nevertheless a very good thing."[29] The Negroes were fond of ornaments, said one Colonel Phipps, "and he appealed to the observation of every gentleman, whether it was the characteristic of miserable persons to show a fondness for finery."[30]

Powerful replies by Pitt, Fox, William Smith, and Philip Francis brought the opposition to its senses. In a long, detailed, and able speech Sir William Young pointed out several errors in the evidence and reasoning of the abolitionists and brought up the unanswerable argument of foreign competition. Contrary to Wilberforce's assertions, he said, France and Spain would never follow England's example; they had plainly evinced their desire to take over the slave trade. That was enough. Despite a last eloquent appeal by Pitt, the House by a vote of 163 to 88 refused leave to introduce a bill for abolition.

Some light may be shed on the reasons for this decision by the debates on the Sierra Leone Settlement Bill which took place the following month. Wilberforce and Henry Thornton, the banker, asked for a joint-stock charter to protect the liability of investors in their experimental colony for freed slaves on the west coast of Africa. Slave traders opposed the whole project. But the Society of Planters and Merchants, after studying the bill and receiving assurances that no competition with West Indian products was intended, decided to forego resistance. Sir William Young, Matthew Montague, and Brook Watson, who had helped defeat abolition, now supported the Sierra Leone bill with words of encouragement.[31] Their attitude indicates that they resisted abolition not out of respect for the slave trade, but out of fear of West Indian ruin.[32]

[28]*Ibid.*, 279–281.
[29]*Ibid.*, 281.
[30]*Ibid.*, 335.
[31]*Ibid.*, XXIX, 653–654.
[32]On May 26, 1791 the slave merchants took advantage of a near-empty House to vote down several improvements in that year's renewal of the

Yet even this statement needs to be qualified. Wilberforce maintained that the planters would not attempt to establish conditions permitting a natural increase in the slave population until the supply of new slaves from Africa was prohibited. It was argued, however, that if the slave trade were cut off before such reforms could take effect, there would be a disastrous reduction in the number of slaves, which could ruin the West Indian economy. The obvious compromise was a gradual abolition. If the planters knew that the slave trade would cease by a given date, they could take the steps necessary to make the change harmless. Proper regulations would prevent the dangers attending a last-minute rush for Africans.

By far the most popular plan for gradual abolition involved a tax on imported slaves, to be increased each year until it became prohibitive. The revenue gained would be given as subsidies for raising creole children. The slave trade to foreign colonies would also be stopped. A bill incorporating these ideas was expected by Liverpool merchants before 1789.[33] Similar plans were suggested to Wilberforce by George Rose,[34] and to a Commons committee on the slave trade by Thomas Irving, Inspector-General of Imports and Exports.[35] Several members of Parliament had expressed their hope for a gradual abolition, and even the City of Bristol agreed in principle.[36]

Wilberforce could not disregard these feelings after his crushing defeat in 1791. After rejecting a plan to martyr himself in the interest of publicity,[37] he decided to go ahead with a new abolition measure designed to conciliate his more moderate opponents. The usual campaign devices were adapted to the

---

Slave Trade Regulating Act. Charles Long, a West Indian, acted as teller in the division against Newnham and Gascoyne.

[33]BM Add MS 38416, 166, Edgar Corrie to Hawkesbury.
[34]Leveson V. Harcourt, ed., *The Diaries and Correspondence of the Right Hon. George Rose* (2 vols., London, 1860), I, 38–39.
[35]*HC Sess Pap* 1790-1(748)XXXIV, 271. Irving supplied trade statistics for all the abolition debates.
[36]*House of Commons Journals*, May 12, 1789, Petition of Mayor, Burgesses and Commonality of Bristol.
[37]The idea was to court a quick defeat for immediate abolition early in 1792 with the hope of arousing public sympathy sufficient to pass another bill later in the session. *Life of Wilberforce*, I, 333.

purpose: "The terms of your petition," he wrote to Thomas Gisborne, "ought to be such as to allow of a man's signing it who rather recoils from the idea of immediate abolition."[38]

Almost before the campaign was begun, however, the news of war in St. Domingue threatened to stop it completely. Wilberforce had to put off his motion for another two months, hoping the situation would improve.

When he finally spoke to the House on April 2, 1792, he "professed himself desirous of now holding no other language than that of conciliation." He asked only for a resolution that the slave trade "ought to be abolished." No date was mentioned.[39] His whole speech was designed to condemn the trade without touching in any way upon the character of the planters. Almost immediately, however, his opponents reversed the emphasis by turning the debate into yet another defense of the planters' respectability. Wilberforce lost the initiative, and it seemed as though he was headed for a second resounding defeat.

Then Henry Dundas spoke. As Secretary of State for the Home Department, President of the East India Company Board of Control, political manager of Scotland and one of Pitt's closest advisors, Dundas combined a wide-ranging knowledge of public affairs with the most powerful individual parliamentary interest then existing. He controlled much of the patronage in both ends of the Empire[40] and influenced the votes of thirty-four Scots M. P.'s and eleven Scots peers.[41] Although he had expressed reservations about Wilberforce's campaign style, no one really knew where he stood on the question of abolition.[42] Illness had prevented his participation in previous debates.

[38]*Ibid.*, 337.
[39]Cobbett, *Parl. Hist.*, XXIX, 1055–1057.
[40]He had the right of appointment to certain offices in the West Indies as well as in India. Cf. Holden Furber, *The Life of Henry Dundas, Viscount Melville, 1742–1811* (Oxford, 1931), 30–31.
[41]*Ibid.*, 228, 235–236.
[42]Although Dundas handled colonial affairs as Home Secretary, he had no intimate relations with the West Indian societies. Cyril Matheson, *The Life of Henry Dundas, First Viscount Melville* (London, 1933), 160.

Now he professed himself friendly to abolition. The African trade was indeed not founded on good policy. It was not essential to the preservation of the West Indies, and the loss of population consequent on its abolition need not be harmful. But, Dundas asked, was immediate abolition tolerable to those most nearly concerned, whose life-long habits were attuned to a commerce encouraged by Parliament? Would not the planters take to smuggling slaves if the trade were abolished without their consent? The present motion was a mistake. "It was in the shape of regulations only that they could totally abolish the African slave trade; and not less speedily, nay, even more speedily, than in the manner which had been proposed." He meant regulations to improve living conditions and to educate Negro children, so that eventually a society of educated, able, free, and loyal native workers would come into being in the West Indies. Dundas was looking far into the future, and he appealed to all men of moderate views to join him in realizing his vision. As a first step, he moved to insert the word "gradually" into Wilberforce's motion for abolition.[43]

In a way no abolitionist had dared to do, Dundas had openly explored the long-range prospects of West Indian society. He accepted emancipation (which Wilberforce feared to mention) as the ultimate goal, and argued that abolition was only one in a series of measures which ought to be taken to realize it. His regulations included much that was done for the slaves, with or without legislation, in the next forty years.

The question of his sincerity will never be settled. Despite the bitter attacks of abolitionists[44] and the rejoinders from Dundas's biographers, there is little evidence on which to base an objective conclusion. Whatever his motives, Dundas received substantial support for his proposal from many parts of the House. All those whose fear of injuring private property had prevented them from accepting abolition now saw the

[43] Cobbett, *Parl. Hist.*, XXIX, 1104–1110.
[44] Thirty years later, forgetting the hopelessness of his position in 1792, Wilberforce maintained that Dundas's intervention was the chief cause of his defeat. Cf. *Life of Wilberforce*, I, 352.

conflict resolved.⁴⁵ Speaker Henry Addington professed himself "immensely relieved and excited."⁴⁶

The abolitionists resolutely attacked Dundas for compromising a sacred principle. The defenders of the slave trade, on the other hand, said little. Some of their arguments had been accepted and others undermined by the concern shown for planters' interests. It was left to Robert Banks Jenkinson, Hawkesbury's son, to attempt a diversion by putting forth harmless alternative regulations.⁴⁷

Jenkinson's motion was defeated 234 to 87. Dundas's amendment gained a majority of 193 to 125, and the amended resolution in favor of gradual abolition was passed 230 to 85. No definite conclusions can be drawn from these figures, other than that the House was unusually well-attended for 6:30 in the morning. It might be suggested, however, that those who voted for Jenkinson's motion opposed the amended resolution, and about forty members voted for the gradual abolition after opposing Dundas's amendment.⁴⁸

So far the House had passed only a resolution stating that gradual abolition of the slave trade was desirable. On April 4, two days after Dundas had proposed his amendment, Wilberforce asked him what he intended to do about it. Dundas replied that Wilberforce should bring in his original bill and leave it to be altered as the House saw fit. Thereafter the cooperation of the West Indian legislatures would have to be gained, in order to make the measure effective. Charles James

⁴⁵In 1802 George Canning appealed "to all those moderate men ... who hailed that proposition (the resolution of 1792) as the first moderate practical measure which had been brought foreward for the sanction of parliament...." Cobbett, *Parl. Hist.*, XXXVI, 861.

⁴⁶*Ibid.*, XXIX, 1110.

⁴⁷Jenkinson offered a motion designed to reward planters who promoted the breeding of slaves, and African traders who imported young female slaves for child-bearing purposes. Cobbett, *Parl. Hist.*, XXIX, 1132–1133.

⁴⁸If it were assumed that the pro-slave trade members voted for Jenkinson's harmless alternatives, and that they were joined by staunch abolitionists in opposing Dundas's amendment, the relative size of the factions might be calculated roughly at 40 abolitionists, 85 anti-abolitionists, and 190 moderates. Cf. *Life of Wilberforce*, I, 346.

Fox at once charged that Dundas had deluded the House. Those who had opposed gradual abolition were now being asked to put it into effect with the doubtful cooperation of their worst opponents. The whole scheme was a fraud, an "affront to the nation."[49]

Dundas was certainly vulnerable to such criticism, but his actions are partly understandable. After all, he had merely amended Wilberforce's motion in accordance with the wishes of the House and had suggested certain measures which he thought should accompany, or precede, abolition. A bill detailing those particular measures, if introduced now, might polarize discussion and prevent a real consensus. Wilberforce's resolution could easily be changed in any direction. Only Wilberforce had the time, talents, and independence for leading such a controversial measure to success. Dundas, a political manager, could not afford the luxury of enthusiasm. And were he to offend the West Indian planters, he would lessen the chances of effecting the measure in his role as Colonial Secretary. In the long run Dundas could best aid the abolitionists by remaining a neutral advisor; and this he was determined to do.

At Fox's insistence, Dundas reluctantly submitted his proposals to a committee of the whole House on April 18. He repeated his belief that cooperation with the planters was essential, and on that ground he set the final date for abolition in 1800. In the meantime there were to be limitations and taxes on the importation of male Africans as well as of diseased, aged, or otherwise infertile persons. The slave trade to foreign colonies was to be ended at once, and slaving ships were to be further regulated. A committee for compensating planters and shipowners would be set up. Finally, Dundas asked the House to petition the King to negotiate treaties for international abolition.[50]

Dundas's suggestion for limiting the trade mainly to women and children, logical but hardly humane, was violently attacked by the abolitionists. Immediate and total prohibition

[49] Cobbet, *Parl. Hist.*, XXIX, 1174–1176.
[50] *Ibid.*, XXIX, 1204–1210.

was again called for, and it was agreed to vote on the terminal date of the plan before considering any other business. On April 25, the Earl of Mornington moved the abolition for January 1793, but was defeated. Another motion, for January 1795, was lost in a flood of bickering.[51] Finally, by a vote of 151 to 132, the House approved abolition for January 1, 1796.

Seeing his carefully integrated plan mutilated, Dundas refused to have anything more to do with it. The remaining clauses, "modified" by Pitt to eliminate all references to compensation, were then passed by the House.[52] The bill was sent to the House of Lords on May 3 along with all the evidence collected during the previous three years.

The abolitionists had little hope of further success. The House of Lords was notorious for its "spontaneous dislike of all change",[53] and on this occasion it would be influenced by the known disapproval of the royal family and of a majority in the cabinet.[54] Dundas's influence might have been helpful in the upper House but now it was working for the opposition. The only chance for abolitionist success was to avoid discussion and to bring on an early vote. Then, if the resolutions failed, they could be immediately renewed in the Commons before the session ended.

This maneuver proved to be impossible because Grenville, who was in charge of the resolutions in the upper House, quickly found himself outflanked. Lord Stormont, aided by the fledgling William, Duke of Clarence, summoned the Lords to insist on the right to their own investigation. To vote on

[51]*Ibid.*, XXIX, 1274–1293. Wilberforce, looking over these debates ten years later, said he "would to God... that it were possible to revive in their full force the emotions which were then excited." *Life of Wilberforce*, III, 29.

[52]The completed bill as reported from committee is in *HC Sess Pap* 1791–2(98)XXXIX.

[53]R. Pares, *George III and the Politicians* (Cambridge, 1960), 42. Pares's discussion of the House of Lords is illuminating.

[54]For the royal family, Cf. *Life of Wilberforce*, I, 352. Lord Hawkesbury now led the anti-abolitionists in the Cabinet, and Lord Thurlow was still in office. In addition, a group of peers led by the Duke of Portland had split with Fox and now opposed both abolition and the French Revolution.

the basis of evidence supplied by the Commons, they warned, would set a dangerous constitutional precedent. Previous witnesses had not testified under oath[55] and their accuracy was doubtful. On May 8, Stormont moved

> that this House do forthwith proceed to examine evidence on the subject of the resolutions... and into the present state of the West India islands, the average quantity of sugar and rum that they produce, and the whole of their trade.

Despite Grenville's protest, the motion was carried, 63 to 36.[56] Then Grenville asked for the appointment of a select committee to speed up the hearings. This was criticized by Lord Thurlow and denied by the House. The Archbishop of Canterbury, who voted with Thurlow, wrote to Pitt in deep anxiety: "My vote was given under a strong impression from the Chancellor's solemn statement that an examination before a committee of the Whole House would not be a cause of delay...."[57]

Exactly six days were spent in committee the rest of that session. On May 14, 1792 Edward Law, counsel for the West India Planters and Merchants, led off with a lengthy recital of the whole case against abolition, paying particular attention to legal precedents.[58] His first witness, Lord McCartney, requested the privilege of giving evidence at the table instead of the Bar of the House because he was a peer of Ireland. He cited a precedent from the reign of James II, but as no one could verify it on a moment's notice the proceedings came to a stumbling halt. After a long discussion it was agreed to continue hearing evidence all the following week and three days per week thereafter.[59] Nothing came of this arrangement and on June 5, Grenville gave up. Though he hoped the business

[55]The oath was administered at the Bar of the Lords as in any court of justice, but not in the Commons committees.
[56]*Parliamentary Register*, XXXIII, 382–394.
[57]J. H. Rose, *Life of Pitt*, part I, 471.
[58]Law's speech is in BM Add MS 12433.
[59]*Parliamentary Register*, XXXII, 419.

would be taken up again early next session, he made no move to commit the Lords to such action.⁶⁰

The great debate had been lost. Henceforth, in the face of West Indian maneuvering and the indifference of moderate men, abolitionists were unable to make any headway. In addition, the principles of reform with which abolition was closely associated soon became unpopular, and during the war with France which followed it lost valuable public support.

Before these developments are recorded the work of the West Indian organizations must be noted. They could not hope to match their opponents in the use of petitions. Wilberforce, profiting by his earlier experience in the radical Yorkshire Association, sent out traveling teams to organize the sending of petitions from all over the kingdom. By 1794 the House of Lords had received 742 of them, the Commons even more. West Indians and slave traders deprecated these tactics as fraudulent attempts to undermine the independence of Parliament. Nevertheless, they sent in counter-petitions. Because they could not produce so many, they tried to concentrate them at important moments. For example, on May 20, 1789 just before the House of Commons went into committee on Wilberforce's resolutions, petitions arrived from seventeen different opposition groups, including twelve from Liverpool alone.⁶¹

The circulation of pamphlets and other forms of propaganda was generally slight until the London Society of Planters and Merchants organized a publicity campaign in January, 1792. A sub-committee, appointed four years earlier to direct the parliamentary defense, was enlarged and directed to publish articles and pamphlets favorable to the slave trade. The "trade" rate was again raised to pay expenses. Since the work of this sub-committee has already been examined in detail,⁶² only a

⁶⁰*Ibid.*, 500. He apparently hoped to reopen the debate if, by chance, the session was extended.
⁶¹*House of Commons Journals*, May 20, 1789.
⁶²Ragatz, *Fall of the Planter Class*, 268–271. Cf. his *Guide to the Study of British Caribbean History, including the Abolition and Emancipation Movements* (Washington, D.C., 1930), which describes extant pamphlets and articles. The Minutes of the Slave Trade sub-committee are bound in a separate volume in the West India Committee archives, London.

few observations are needed here. Newspaper editors were paid to insert letters, news, and favorable reports of parliamentary debates. A publicity manager was hired to mount an extensive campaign in the provincial papers, while the West India Society subcommittee prepared answers to abolitionists' pamphlets. When Parliament resumed debate on the slave trade, subcommittee members wrote and approved briefs for both counsel and witnesses before they appeared in either House. On May 7, 1792, the day before gradual abolition was taken up in the Lords, formal letters were sent to all "friendly" peers requesting their attendance at the debate. Finally, after the session had ended, the pamphlets so far published were bound into convenient volumes for distribution to the circulating libraries of all the fashionable watering places.

After 1792 such strenuous efforts were no longer needed. In any event financial troubles limited the work that could be undertaken. By May 1793, the treasury of the London Society of Planters and Merchants was over £600 in debt.[63] After a new appeal for funds, the local sugar factors released £1600 collected under "trade", but no funds came in from the outports. All appeals to Bristol and Glasgow were ignored, and the Liverpool West Indians complained that their contributions had been appropriated by the African merchants' association.[64] During the next four years, planters were repeatedly asked to give particular directions to their outport agents that their "trade" levy must be paid to the London Society. But collections remained nearly two years behind schedule.[65]

Partly in consequence of the lack of funds the avalanche of abolitionist propaganda was never matched. Ragatz located 47 pamphlets published in defense of the slave trade but 109 against it, the latter usually having a larger printing.[66] The West Indians had to concentrate their pamphlets, like their petitions, for maximum effect. Most were sent to members of Parliament, for a very good reason: speakers usually preferred

[63]Min WI Plant, May 18, 1793.
[64]*Ibid.*, June 1, 1793.
[65]*Ibid.*, April 28, 1796.
[66]Ragatz, *Fall of the Planter Class*, 253.

to consult a written brief when standing before either House, but few of them cared to wade through the vast sea of evidence on abolition to collect the necessary materials. Pamphlets were easier to digest and convenient to use. Much of the repetitive quality of the abolition debates may be ascribed to the wide circulation of pamphlets among peers and M. P.'s.

6

The Parliamentary Conflict, 1793-1803

In May 1792 William Pitt issued the first of his proclamations against seditious meetings and publications. During the months that followed, the administration's alarm over the spread of revolutionary sentiment was transmitted to the British public. Parliament was recalled early the following session to consider the advance of the revolutionary armies. On February 11, 1793, George III declared war on the French Republic.

The ideas of political reform with which so many opponents of the slave trade were associated, as well as the methods of propaganda they had developed so skillfully, were now discredited by their apparent derivation from revolutionary France. William Wilberforce, having been declared an honorary citizen of the Republic (much against his will), lost favor with the King[1] and other conservatives. It was natural for abolitionists, who had based their campaign upon the mobilization of public sympathy, to attribute their subsequent failures primarily to the surge of political reaction. Both in their contemporary correspondence and in later memoirs they tended to overlook the strength of the economic and political argu-

[1] Cf. *Dropmore MSS*, II, 308.

ments against abolition, the skill of their opponents, and the mistakes of Wilberforce himself.

Wilberforce approached the parliamentary session of 1792–93 with two handicaps, besides that of anti-Jacobinism derived from his previous anti-slave trade agitation. One was the charge put forward by West Indian planters that abolitionist propaganda had provoked the recent renewal of violence in the French colony of St. Domingue. It will be recalled[2] that French troops arrived in St. Domingue in September 1792 to enforce a decree of racial equality among all free men. When white colonists resisted, their slaves were incited to revolt. Soon the whole colony was disrupted. The Jamaica legislature issued a lengthy condemnation of Wilberforce and all other "seditious innovators" for their alleged interference, making certain that every peer received a copy before hearings on gradual abolition were resumed in the House of Lords.

The second handicap concerned a Captain Kimber, master of a Liverpool slave ship. Kimber had been indicted in the summer of 1792 on the strength of a parliamentary speech by Wilberforce for torturing to death a slave girl while on a voyage from Africa to the West Indies. Abolitionists gave the case wide publicity, but their two principal witnesses were themselves indicted for perjury and Captain Kimber went free.[3] Wilberforce was ridiculed in the press and in Parliament for his part in the affair.

Inhibited, perhaps, by these new developments and by the preparations for war, the Lords spent only five days in committee on the slave trade during the session of 1792–1793. Proceedings did not even begin until after the Easter recess, because counsel for the Society of Planters and Merchants were out on circuit duty.[4] There was no question of indifference, however. When debate finally opened, Lord Abingdon launched

[2]See p. 67.
[3]The Standing Committee of Planters and Merchants allocated £2500 for his legal defense.
[4]*House of Lords Journal*, March 20, 1793. The absence of their counsel was known in advance by the Society of Planters and Merchants and could probably have been avoided.

a violent diatribe against the abolitionists' supposed revolutionary sympathies, and was sharply rebuked by Grenville. The Duke of Clarence, self-appointed representative of the royal family, was forced to apologize for calling Wilberforce "a fanatic or a hypocrite."[5]

Early in the session Wilberforce decided to renew the resolutions for gradual abolition in the House of Commons. If they were passed there, the Lords might feel obligated to speed their own abolition hearings and come to an early decision. This maneuver, coming so soon after the explosion of anti-Jacobinism, the Kimber affair, and the violence in St. Domingue, was certain to meet strong opposition. Furthermore, Wilberforce undertook it only two weeks after war was declared with France, when Parliament and the public were still greatly distracted.

The abolitionist leader regarded his first step, asking for leave to introduce the resolutions, as a mere procedural formality. His speech was unusually brief and few of his supporters bothered to attend. But the opposition were out in force to veto the motion almost before it was recorded.

The Society of Planters and Merchants was now beginning to benefit from the reorganization of its subcommittee on abolition. Most of the Society's members, being resident in or near London, could be reached quickly. Further, their political interest had been quickened by the coming of war to the West Indies. Consequently, when Wilberforce introduced bills later in the session for abolishing the slave trade to foreign territories, and for reducing it to British colonies, there were again enough West Indians on hand to defeat him.[6]

Both in 1793 and 1794 the defenders of the slave trade were

[5]Cobbett, *Parl. Hist.*, XXX, 659–660. The Prince of Wales, reporting to the Duke of York on April 14, said "William (Duke of Clarence) made a *most incomparable speech* on the slave trade on Thursday. . . . Lord Thurlow assured me it was as good as possible." (A. Aspinall, *The Correspondence of George Prince of Wales*, 4 vols., London, 1963–65, II, no. 740.) Debrett, in a rare footnote to his *Parliamentary Register*, XXXVI, 161, said a letter from Lord Stanhope to Condorcet, read by the Duke in his speech, "certainly proved that the ideas of French freedom were connected with the slave trade in this country."
[6]Cobbett, *Parl. Hist.*, XXX 515–516.

spared the eloquent attacks of Pitt. He was, of course, busy directing the war effort. But he was also irked by Wilberforce's constant badgering, as Harriet Martineau has emphasized:[7]

> Wilberforce saw little or nothing beyond the cause to which he had devoted his life; and in the most innocent way, he would endanger the government, and harass the Minister, and push aside all business but his own... and then mourn over the lack of principle and zeal in the Minister who had all the affairs of empire on his hands.

Pitt was also forced to moderate his enthusiasm by political developments which came to a head in July 1794. A reactionary group of opposition peers and M. P.'s, led by the Duke of Portland had split with Fox over his attitude to the French Revolution and was drawn gradually into coalition with Pitt's government. In order to secure the group's forty-odd votes in the Commons,[8] Pitt was constrained to abandon for the time being such liberal projects as parliamentary reform and Catholic emancipation.[9] Abolition of the slave trade was also subject to negotiation:

> On Lord Loughborough's observing to him that... the strong manner in which he (Pitt) had promoted the abolition of the Slave Trade, would require some explanation, he said, certainly some concessions must be made; the King did not like the measure, still less the manner in which it was supported by addresses and petitions, a method he (Pitt) also disliked, as it was a bad precedent to establish.[10]

Thus the Prime Minister could not support Wilberforce's attempts to put pressure on the Lords, and Lord Grenville's

---

[7] Harriet Martineau, *An Introduction to the History of England during the Thirty Years' Peace* (2 vols., London, 1851), I, clviii.

[8] Portland told Dundas in January 1793 that he could bring forty to fifty M. P.'s over to Government. Malmesbury, *The Diary and Correspondence of James Harris, First Earl of Malmesbury* (2 vols., London, 1844), II, 501.

[9] G. M. Trevelyan, *Lord Grey of the Reform Bill* (London, 1929), 55.

[10] Malmesbury, *Diary and Correspondence*, II, 463-464.

effectiveness in that House was seriously compromised because five strong opponents of abolition had now joined the administration.[11] Only three days were given by the Lords for hearing evidence on abolition during the session of 1794.[12] The only one of the 1792 resolutions with any chance of success now was that for abolishing the slave trade to foreign colonies. In fact it had become partly superfluous, for British slave ships dared not enter the zones of French naval activity in the Caribbean and some were even captured by French privateers while still on the coast of Africa. It was in order to perpetuate this slump in trade that Wilberforce re-introduced the resolution against trading with foreigners on February 7, 1794. His opponents had no defense. The old arguments in favor of revenue and established trade were not applicable, while every reference to "French principles" merely dramatized the bill's value as a weapon of economic warfare.[13] It was passed by a vote of 56 to 38 in the House of Commons.

Three months elapsed before the measure was brought up for its second reading in the upper House. During the interval Tobago, Martinique, St. Lucia, and Guadaloupe were all captured from the French. Troops were sent from England to attempt a re-conquest of St. Domingue in the interest of Jamaican security. The terms of surrender offered the French colonists included guarantees of equal treatment with the British in the slave trade. Thus the foreign slave trade bill pending in Parliament was deprived of its effectiveness. Most of the peers, moreover, disliked taking action on a partial abolition while the main question was still being debated. They decided, as usual, to postpone the whole business for another session.[14]

The proceedings of 1794 should have convinced Wilberforce

[11]The Duke of Portland, Lord Loughborough, and Lords Fitzwilliam, Malmesbury, and Carlisle.
[12]The sixteen witnesses examined by the Lords, 1792-1794, were all opposed to abolition.
[13]Cutting off the supply of slaves could hinder colonial production, the transport of which was considered a primary source of French maritime strength.
[14]Cobbett, *Parl. Hist.*, XXXI, 467-470.

that measures of restriction or partial abolition had a greater chance of success than his original bill. After all, the Lords regularly renewed the Slave Trade Regulating Act with no hesitation. A similar compromise, possibly concerning the treatment of slaves in the West Indies, might receive wide support. But Wilberforce was still captivated by the 1792 resolutions. He insisted upon a quick and complete abolition and moved another declaration to that effect in Parliament in February 1795.

By that time he was again in political hot water. His growing opposition to the War had moved Pitt, in January, to break off their life-long friendship. Fox thought Wilberforce would join his opposition party. Instead he steered a middle course, affronted both sides, and was even suspected of trying to raise a third party. "The bulk of the people think you are doing a great deal of mischief," warned the Dean of Carlisle.[15]

Pitt, much to his credit, came down to the House to support the motion for immediate abolition in 1795. But Henry Dundas came too, arguing that more time was needed by planters, who under wartime conditions were unable to build up a stock of slaves sufficient to cushion the shock of abolition. The House was also assured by Sir William Young, who had recently visited the islands, that independent efforts now being made by the planters would make the slave trade unnecessary "in a few years." The motion for abolition was defeated, 78–61.[16]

To what extent was anti-Jacobinism contributing to Wilberforce's failure in Parliament? The proceedings from 1793 through 1795 certainly show that the House of Lords was hostile to abolition, and that it noticed the abolitionists' affinities with revolutionary agitators. But though the latter characteristic may have strengthened the former it did not cause it. The House of Lords had been almost as antipathetic to regulating the slave trade in 1788, before the French Revolution. It also had a long record of opposition to all great reforms, a record which several abolitionists noted with despair before anti-Jacobinism ever appeared.

[15] *Life of Wilberforce*, II, 72–76.
[16] Cobbett, *Parl. Hist.*, XXXI, 1321–1345.

A similar comparison might be made for the House of Commons. The defeats of 1793–1795 were far less decisive than that of 1791, when Wilberforce had had public opinion on his side. Moreover, in 1794 the Commons did pass a bill for prohibiting the slave trade to foreign territories, despite vigorous accusations of sedition by the West Indians. Thus the primacy of anti-Jacobinism among obstacles to abolition cannot be accepted as a valid interpretation.

In any event the Commons' votes on abolition between 1792 and 1800 were too small to be analysed in general terms. Most of the M. P.'s, through hostility, indifference, or a sense of futility, did not bother to attend the House when the question was discussed. Success or failure often depended on the few men who chanced to be present, or within hailing distance, at the time a division occurred.

This observation is most clearly illustrated by the debates of 1796. On February 18 Wilberforce again called for immediate abolition and this time brought in all his supporters to ensure a favorable reception to his bill. The precaution was wise, for Lord Penrhyn had ordered the secretary of the Standing Committee of Planters and Merchants to send letters to all friendly M. P.'s asking their attendance. The motion for leave to introduce the bill therefore occasioned a direct test of numerical strength. Ninety-three votes were cast for abolition, sixty-seven against. The "Cause" was not so hopeless as its advocates afterwards liked to assert.

On Monday, February 22, Wilberforce found the House "in a good state", brought in his bill, and obtained an unopposed first reading. But on March 3, while he was dining with a party of abolitionists, an opponent moved the second reading, hoping to defeat the bill in a thinly-attended House. Wilberforce discovered the trick in time, hurried to his seat, spoke until his friends came, and carried the second reading 64 to 31.[17]

Four days later the bill was put into committee by a vote of 76 to 31. Pro-slave trade members, unable to muster enough

[17] *Life of Wilberforce*, II, 141. Cobbett, *Parl. Hist.*, XXXII, 862, does not say who moved the second reading, but both Tarleton and Young spoke against it.

sympathetic allies, spoke as though the bill were certain to pass.[18] But when the committee's report came up for approval on March 15, everything changed. The defense had regrouped its forces, while Wilberforce's supporters had begun to relax. Ten or twelve of the latter went out of town, others to the opera.[19] The principal speaker for the opposition was Henry Dundas, now at the height of his political power. The votes he controlled may well have proved decisive for the bill was lost by a narrow margin, 74 to 70.[20]

The defenders of the slave trade could hardly feel satisfied. Only a generous piece of luck had saved them in the Commons. Next time some form of abolition was almost sure to pass; and the House of Lords, having abandoned its enquiry into the general question, could not again refuse to consider a specific bill. A hard-line defense was no longer safe. The West Indians would have to take the initiative and offer concessions liberal enough to attract moderate M. P.'s, but not too liberal for the colonial legislatures.

Hints of the West Indians' new way of thinking[21] appeared quickly. On March 22, 1796, the Standing Committee of Planters and Merchants thanked Dundas for his recent "effectual opposition" to the abolition bill. At the same time it asked him to send an outline of his plan "for the future Regulation of the Slave Trade", which apparently aimed at gradual abolition.[22]

Three weeks later Dundas joined the West Indians to oppose a bill brought in by Philip Francis which sought to increase fertility and productivity among the slaves by promoting marriage and by alloting them private tracts of arable land. The obvious aim was a gradual abolition, but the critics did not object to that. Instead they deplored the assumption that Parliament could meddle with the internal affairs of the colonies without asking the cooperation of either the legislatures or the

[18]Cobbett, *Parl. Hist.*, XXXII, 863–865.
[19]*Life of Wilberforce*, II, 142.
[20]A list of the abolitionist minority is given at the end of the report in Cobbett, *Parl. Hist.*, XXXIII, 901.
[21]There is no evidence that the Liverpool M. P.'s were involved.
[22] Min WI Plant, March 22, 1796.

planters themselves. Such an approach, in their view, was fruitless and unconstitutional.[23]

Philip Francis's bill was quickly defeated, but it raised one issue which had not been considered since the debates of 1792. The important question was this: should the African trade be abolished in order to effect an improvement in West Indian slave conditions or *vice versa?* The answer depended upon one's view, which had never been clearly ascertained, of the planters' willingness to cooperate. If they could accept a program of reform leading gradually to abolition, they would have the support of a majority in Parliament. If not, then moderate men would swing behind Wilberforce.

Sir William Young had once said that abolition would come, in the end, from the West Indies. Now he determined to put his ideas to the test. He approached Charles Rose Ellis, another prominent West Indian,[24] and together they organized a "Society of West Indian Landholders in Parliament," which was to meet on December 14, 1796. Before the meeting, Young and Ellis prepared an analysis of the future prospects for abolition, basing their report on a communication from the St. Vincent's legislature.[25] The conclusions of the report are crucial to an understanding of moderate West Indian thinking:

> 1st. That the repeated discussion of the abolition of the Slave Trade in Parliament, may produce consequences of the utmost danger to the Colonies, and that if an Act for this purpose should ever pass the British Parliament, it will be fatal to them.
>
> 2nd. That the question of abolition will continue to be agitated year after year, and as often as the forms of the House permit, and that neither the House of Commons

[23]Cobbett, *Parl. Hist.*, XXXII, 944–992.
[24]Charles Rose Ellis (1771–1845), created Baron Seaford in 1826, was the scion of a wealthy family established in Jamaica since 1665. He entered the House of Commons in March, 1793 at the age of 21. Not a brilliant speaker, he attached himself through his cousin George Ellis to George Canning and eventually became acknowledged head of the West Indian interest in Parliament.
[25]Cf. *HC Sess Pap* 1803–4(119)X, "Report of a Committee of the St. Vincent's Assembly."

nor the Country in general, will suffer it to rest 'till some steps have been taken which may afford them reason to believe that every Regulation has been adopted, which is consistent with the safety of the Colonies.

3rd. That many persons of great weight and character, tho' conscious of the danger to be apprehended from the measures proposed by Mr. Wilberforce, have supported, and will continue to support them, because no mode of conduct at all compatible with their ideas of humanity has been proposed as an alternative.

4th. That on the other hand many persons who have hitherto opposed the measures of Mr. Wilberforce will feel themselves under the necessity of submitting to them, unless some plan of regulation shall be brought forward.

5th. That there is reason to believe, that besides Mr. Wilberforce's Bill, there will be proposed some more specious plan of moderate reform and gradual abolition, which will meet with very general support, and that it is of the utmost importance that such a plan should be anticipated, because the West India Proprietors from their local knowledge, are the only persons to whom the formation of it can be safely entrusted.

6th. That consequently, for the joint purposes of opposing the plan of Mr. Wilberforce, and establishing the Character of the West India Body, it is essential that they should manifest their willingness to promote actively the cause of Humanity by such steps as shall be consistent with safety to the property of Individuals and the general interests of the Colonies.

7th. That to reconcile the rights of Colonial Legislatures with the necessity of some proceeding in Parliament, [the Committee proposes a motion to be put before Parliament], "That an humble Address be presented to His Majesty, requesting that His Majesty will be graciously pleased to give Directions to the Governors of His Majesty's

Plantations in the West Indies, to recommend to the respective Councils and Assemblies of the said Plantations to adopt such Measures as shall appear to them best calculated to obviate the Causes which have hitherto impeded the natural Increase of the Negroes already in the islands, gradually to diminish the necessity of the Slave Trade, and ultimately to lead to its complete termination; and particularly, with a view to the same effect, to employ such means as may conduce to the Moral & Religious Improvement of the Negroes, and secure to them throughout all the West India Islands, the certain, immediate, and active protection of the Law; and at the same time, assuring His Majesty, that this House will concur in such Measures as shall appear requisite to be taken by this House for the attainment of the same object.[26]

The report was "highly approved of" by twenty-one M.P.'s at the meeting of December 14. Charles Ellis was requested to present the motion to Parliament, and it was further agreed "that Mr. Ellis and Sir William Young do wait on Mr. Dundas, and submit the motion to his consideration."[27]

Ellis brought in his motion for an address on April 6, 1797. After reciting the arguments against an immediate abolition and the natural difficulties of maintaining the slave population by natural means, he announced his intention of ending the slave trade by making it unnecessary, with the cooperation of the colonial legislatures. Joseph Foster Barham, a West Indian merchant, seconded the motion with a perceptive interrogation of Parliament's past attitude. Noting the insults which had been heaped upon the planters, he asked "Could anything be expected from such treatment but the consequence that has ensued, namely, a determined resistance to everything that was proposed from the same quarter?"[28]

The point was not lost on moderate abolitionists. Wilber-

[26]From Young's letter to the Leeward Islands Assembly, CO 152:78, 221 ff.
[27]*Ibid.*, 222.
[28]Cobbett, *Parl. Hist.*, XXXIII, 273–274.

force once noted that many of them had become nauseated by the unceasing invective with which the cause was promoted. Now they were offered a chance to wipe the slate clean, to act on a basis of understanding and cooperation with the planters. It was, as Young had hoped, just what they wanted. Dundas gave his full support, and the address was approved by a vote of 99 to 63.[29]

Wilberforce and Fox offered frantic opposition. They were convinced that the address was merely a pretext for delay and that the planters would never cooperate. On the first count they were wrong, at least in regard to Ellis and Young. On the second they were right. But had they foreseen the consequences of the planters' resistance, they might not have been so despondent.

Ellis's address passed easily through the House of Lords. Even the reactionary Duke of Portland, now personally interested in the West Indies,[30] professed to be satisfied. In his capacity as Colonial Secretary[31] he sent the address to the colonial governors for presentation to their respective legislatures, adding on his own initiative "such ideas, as I conceived would have an immediate tendency to promote those desirable objects."[32] George Chalmers's message to the Bahamas was in a similar vein: "This event will now lead on very properly to your intended act, for meliorating the condition of your Slaves...."[33] On the whole, it seemed a promising start.

But as answers were returned by the several West Indian legislatures during the next few years, it became apparent that the resident planters had no intention of ending the slave trade. A committee of the Jamaica House of Assembly reported in

[29]*Ibid.*, 294. A proposed amendment, to delete all reference to ending the slave trade, was vetoed without a division.

[30]He had obtained the reversions to valuable offices in the West Indies for many of his nephews and grandsons. A. P. Thornton, *The Habit of Authority* (London, 1966), 121.

[31]Portland took over the Home Office with its colonial business in 1794, when Dundas became the new Secretary of State for War. In 1801 colonial affairs were transferred to the War Office.

[32]CO 152:78, 295. Portland to President Thompson of Antigua, August 1798.

[33]BM Add MS 22900, 331.

1800 that "everything possible" had already been done "to render the condition of the slaves therein as favourable as is consistent with their reasonable services, and the safety of the white inhabitants."[34] In newly-captured Trinidad, Governor Thomas Picton issued an "Ordnance for Regulating the Treatment of Slaves" which advised the planters of their duties; but its loose construction and vague penalty clauses rendered it almost useless.[35] A more elaborate and subtle response came from the General Council and Assembly of the Leeward Islands, meeting in March 1798. Before taking any action on the ideas communicated by Ellis, Portland and Young, the Council passed nine resolutions outlining its constant efforts to promote the welfare of slaves and condemning the fraudulent and dangerous interference of abolitionists. The Council promised to frame new laws for the comfort and moral improvement of the slaves, "with the pleasing hope, that among other happy consequences their numbers may encrease [sic], and the necessity of the Slave Trade cease to exist." But it added this stern qualification:[36]

> ... upon the whole, whatever measures we are induced to take for the melioration of the condition of Slaves, proceed chiefly from motives of humanity, and a disposition to promote His Majesty's benevolent views in their favor, and not from any prospect of an immediate termination of the Slave Trade; which at present is essentially necessary to the existence of these colonies.

As might have been expected, the laws passed by the Leeward Islands legislature in 1798 were liberal in tone but conservative in effect. None of them made any reference, even in their preambles, to the possibility of ending the importation of Africans.

[34]Thomas Southey, *Chronological History of the West Indies*, III, 173 quoted in Sir Alan Burns, *History of the British West Indies* (London, 1954), 559.
[35]CO 295:14, located after Picton's letter of April 30, 1806. All West Indian slave laws were difficult to enforce because local courts did not accept evidence from Negroes, whether slave or free, against a white offender.
[36]CO 152:78, 211–212.

Moreover, the Leeward Islands Council followed Jamaica's lead[37] in asserting that Parliament had no right to legislate on a subject of such importance to the colonies' internal prosperity.

The disappointing response from the West Indies was not made known to Parliament until 1804. In the meantime, further abolitionist legislation was discouraged both by the existence of Ellis's address and by the increasingly conservative tone of the Cabinet brought about by the Portland group. Anti-slave trade M. P.'s found the situation in the House of Commons almost hopeless. In May 1797 a disgusted Wilberforce wrote a letter to his lawyer rather than listen to the West Indians rip apart his new motion for immediate abolition.[38] Within a few days, the Foxite Whigs seceded from Parliament in protest at the government's policy of reaction. They came back on April 3, 1798 to support Wilberforce in a division, but even though Dundas was missing they could give little help. Leave to bring in a bill for abolition was vetoed, 87 to 83, because, wrote Sir William Young, "we had with us sense, justice, policy, & *every good feeling*. . . . ."[39]

The following year, 1799, was filled with abolitionist projects. Dolben's Slave Trade Regulating Act was strengthened with further amendments and given permanent status. However, a bill introduced by Henry Thornton to prohibit the slave trade in the vicinity of the experimental colony at Sierra Leone on the African coast failed at the last moment. It was passed by the Commons despite strong objections from Liverpool. On its second reading in the Lords, however, the Duke of Clarence,[40] together with "some of the members of Administration, who are supported by a great appearance of Court Influence",[41] put

[37] On two occasions, in 1792 and 1799, the Jamaicans infuriated Henry Dundas by criticizing in no uncertain terms Parliament's interference in their domestic concerns.
[38] *Life of Wilberforce*, II, 218.
[39] CO 261:9, 148. Young's emphasis.
[40] The Common Council of Liverpool presented the Duke with the freedom of the borough, "in grateful sense of his active and able exertions" on behalf of the slave trade. Gomer Williams, *History of the Liverpool Privateers*, 618.
[41] PRO 30/8:101, 143–144: Pitt to Lord Chatham, May 29, 1799. Pitt told Wilberforce that the King himself had not influenced the voting.

up a stout resistance. The abolitionists might have won even then, had not Lord Grenville made a disastrous mistake concerning proxy votes. The bill was defeated, 68 to 63.[42]

The session of 1799 is however chiefly notable for an attempt at further compromise on abolition carried out behind the scenes, which was apparently wrecked by intransigent absentee planters and members of the royal family. The pattern of events, though not entirely clear, is important enough to warrant a tentative reconstruction.

On June 7, 1799, George Canning wrote his friend Wilbraham Bootle, one of the moderates who voted against immediate abolition but favored a gradual approach. Canning said he had planned to bring in a bill to limit the importation of Africans to the annual decrease in the West Indian slave population, and to prohibit the clearing of new land for cultivation with slave labor. "The Ellises and Edwards were decidedly with me.... Dundas and Windham on the one side agreed to the compromise and Wilberforce on the other...."[43] But Pitt finally decided that his own prestige, together with the necessity of preventing further scandalous opposition in the House of Lords, demanded that the plan be discussed in the Cabinet, made into a government measure, and passed on the strength of official support.[44] Accordingly the prime minister gave notice of his intent to introduce a bill on the slave trade. And he called a Cabinet meeting for July 9 to discuss the matter.

Before the meeting Pitt outlined his intentions in a letter to Charles Jenkinson, now Lord Liverpool,[45] whose concurrence would be highly important. "I know how much we differ on the general Question," he said, "but these Ideas appear to me to

[42]*Life of Wilberforce*, II, 340.

[43]The Ellises and Edwards were West Indian families; William Windham had been an abolitionist, but reversed his position after joining the government with the Duke of Portland. The assertion of Wilberforce's approval is apparently correct: see the *Life of Wilberforce*, II, 367–368 for a letter which may refer to Canning's ideas.

[44]Captain Josceline Bagot, ed., *George Canning and His Friends* (2 vols., London, 1909), I, 149–152.

[45]Not to be confused with his son Robert, the later prime minister, now known by the courtesy title of Lord Hawkesbury. Charles Jenkinson was created first Earl of Liverpool in 1796.

rest on such separate grounds, that I do not despair of our being nearer as Agreement on them."[46] Unfortunately, Pitt was mistaken. Lord Liverpool replied that he was too sick to come to town (which may have been true: he suffered from gout), but in any event he did not feel justified in pledging himself to any proposition that might affect the property of His Majesty's subjects.[47] The "King's Friend" then wrote an explanation to the Duke of Clarence:[48]

> As Lord Liverpool understood from His Royal Highness, that it was the King's determination that any business of this sort should never be made a cabinet measure, he thought he should act contrary to His Majesty's intentions, if he was present at this Cabinet.

Lord Liverpool may have been misled by the Duke of Clarence, who was prone to falsehoods and disliked by his father.[49] In this case George III accepted Pitt's promise that everyone would be allowed to judge for himself, and the compromise bill was laid before the Cabinet with his consent.[50]

The Cabinet meeting of July 9 was reported to Lord Liverpool by the Duke of Portland, who complimented his ally on the defense of "the old true policy of our ancestors:"

> ... Mr. Pitt opened the business very little farther than in his letter to you, and with great [illegible] respect to contrary opinions, and a declaration that nothing was farther from his intention than to pledge any of the persons present to that or any other measure of the kind. Of this, Ld. Westmoreland, Dundas & myself availed our-

---

[46] BM Add MS 38192, 102.
[47] BM Add MS 38416, 311. Liverpool to the Duke of Clarence, July 8, 1799.
[48] *Ibid.*, 312. He asked the Duke to inform the King of his loyal conduct, lest it be misrepresented by others.
[49] Cf. A. Aspinall, *The Correspondence of George Prince of Wales* (2 vols., London, 1962–3), II, #599, and I, #262 and #266.
[50] BM Add MS 38190, 108.

selves, and it was stated & admitted to be merely a communication of which he (Mr. Pitt) thought himself called upon to do in consequence of the notice he had given to the H. of Commons.[51]

Pitt's position was most frustrating. His every attempt at reasonable discussion of slave trade legislation was defeated by prejudice. He had no real party of his own to back him,[52] and his old weapon against the King, the threat of resignation, was useless so long as the hated alternative government (the Foxites) remained out of Parliament.[53] Wilberforce wished Pitt to proceed with the compromise bill without Cabinet support. But before anything could be settled, a general meeting of the Society of Planters and Merchants condemned the compromise with such force that all the moderate West Indians, except Sir William Young, withdrew their support. Pitt was obliged to suspend his initiative. His reputation suffered because the public knew about the intended bill, although not about the negotiations for it. Later in 1799 Canning advised Pitt that "very many friends doubted whether he now desired to carry abolition, while some even commended his prudence in doing less than he professed in the matter."[54]

The Prime Minister had no further chance to redeem himself. Indeed, before he went out of office he had another misunderstanding with Wilberforce. The abolitionist leader had been promised an Order-in-Council prohibiting the enormous slave trade to colonies conquered by the British during the war.[55] He learned, however, that Pitt had accepted an argument of the planters, that slaves already purchased could be transferred to the new settlements under the classification of fixed capital investments. The West Indian community was in high spirits

[51] BM Add MS 38191, 245-246.
[52] "At the end of seventeen years' undisputed preeminence he commanded no more than fifty or sixty personal followers." R. Pares, *George III and the Politicians*, 78.
[53] G. M. Trevelyan, *Lord Grey of the Reform Bill*, 99.
[54] J. H. Rose, *The Life of Pitt*, part I, 477.
[55] *Life of Wilberforce*, II, 368.

over this compromise. After a long argument, Wilberforce succeeded in getting the agreement withdrawn, but the original Order-in-Council was shelved as well.

In February, 1801 Pitt was replaced as prime minister by his protégé, Henry Addington. The new administration was top-heavy with anti-abolitionists,[56] and the character of the new head of government did nothing to brighten Wilberforce's hopes. Addington's two biographers agree that he was in favor of abolition but was too cautious, too respectful of established interests, and too responsive to the King's wishes to take initiative in the matter.[57] When Canning and Wilberforce pressed him in the House of Commons, he promised to appoint a committee on gradual abolition.[58] But the renewal of war in 1803 caused this plan to be postponed.

For various reasons Wilberforce was unable to bring forward a bill of his own. In any event, he knew he would probably not receive a hearing. In addition to enemies in the Cabinet, there were 100 new Irish members, brought into Parliament by the Act of Union in 1801, whose opinions on abolition for the time being were largely negative.[59]

Thus after fifteen years of campaigning only two measures concerning the slave trade had passed both Houses of Parliament. One was the Regulating Act of 1788, which was now permanently established. The other was Ellis's address to the King in 1797. Wilberforce had had nothing to do with either of them: his personal record was one of almost complete failure.

He did not realize that the West Indians had come to the end of their rope. Ellis's address, despite the enthusiasm with which

[56]Lord Pelham, Home Secretary for two years, was the only avowed abolitionist. Lord Chatham was doubtful, Lord Hobart apparently indifferent. The rest were hostile to abolition. Wilberforce noted (*Life of Wilberforce*, III, 2) that young Hawkesbury at the Foreign Office would be "the main pillar" of the administration. Lord Liverpool also remained as President of the Committee for Trade.

[57]George Pellew, *The Life and Correspondence of the Rt. Hon. Henry Addington, 1st Viscount Sidmouth* (3 vols., London, 1847), II 430, 447; and Philip Ziegler, *Addington* (London, 1965), 151 and *passim*.

[58]Cobbett, *Parl. Hist.*, XXXVI, 878–880.

[59]Cf. *Life of Wilberforce*, III, 88.

it was launched, failed completely to bring about its principal objects. As soon as this fact was made known to Parliament the planters were sure to lose much support. More important, however, the whole foundation of West Indian commerce, on which the defense of the slave trade ultimately rested, was crumbling. And the war, which had once hampered the cause of abolition, was now working in its favor. It is worth examining these developments in detail before considering further the parliamentary defense of the British slave trade.

7

War and Trade in the West Indies 1792-1804

Most members of Parliament recognized three principal objections to the immediate abolition of the British slave trade. First, it might seriously impair the capacity of the British West Indies to raise crops for export, especially sugar, which provided revenues for government and incomes for investors. Secondly, by ruining the West Indies abolition might destroy a valuable market for British manufactures and plantation supplies, as well as the shipping involved with that trade. Thirdly, a unilateral abolition would merely transfer the slaves and the whole African commerce to foreign merchants, with a consequent loss of revenue and navigation but with no compensating relief for the Africans themselves.

Beginning in 1793 each of these objections was gradually undermined by political and economic developments related to the war with France. By 1804 none of them was valid. The British West Indies had become so economically embarrassed that a reduction of their capacity, and that of their rivals, for growing sugar was considered essential. Foreign merchants had been driven out of the African trade so that a unilateral abolition by Britain seemed potentially more effective. Finally, by 1804 British merchants and shipowners had lost much of their

Caribbean trade to American interlopers as a result of the planters' demands for cheap supplies and were no longer so enthusiastic about fighting abolition.

During the half-century before 1792 the world supply of sugar increased more rapidly than the demand. British Caribbean planters, whose command of capital had enabled them to expand production at an early date, saw their advantage gradually whittled away by French, Spanish, Portuguese, and Scandinavian rivals. The foreigners usually stayed on their plantations to reduce the costs of overhead and inefficiency. They had direct access to continental markets, whereas British sugar was always transshipped through London or Bristol; and the foreigners enjoyed preferential tariffs in their own mother countries. In addition, after 1783 foreign colonists were allowed to buy cheap provisions in America, a privilege denied to the British. All these differences were reflected in continental markets, where British sugar was consistently undersold by competitors.

Until 1787 Parliament subsidized re-exports of British sugar in order to improve the balance of trade. Muscovado (brown) sugar paid import duties totaling 11 shillings per hundredweight (cwt.) on arrival in England, but gained a "drawback" or bounty of 12s. 4d. per cwt. if subsequently exported. This subsidy enabled British sugar factors to sell excess sugar on the Continent so that prices would remain high in England. Grocers and sugar refiners protested the practice but were unable to defeat the West Indian interest in Parliament.

The import duties on British sugar occasionally caused trouble to West Indian planters because they were calculated by weight rather than by price. This meant that low-priced sugar paid proportionately higher duties than expensive kinds. Whenever there was a general slump in prices, British planters were hit especially hard.

Between 1783 and 1792 the lack of an adequate outlet on the Continent caused British wholesale sugar prices to decline steadily. West Indian planters, already in a weakened economic position,[1] were threatened with bankruptcy. Only major re-

[1]See pp. 8–14.

forms in agricultural production, or a major stroke of luck, could save them. Luck, it seemed, was the answer, for in 1792 the French colony of St. Domingue was destroyed by revolution. In 1791 St. Domingue had been the largest and most productive sugar colony in the world. She contained as many Negro slaves and exported as much sugar as all the British West Indies combined.[2] Moreover, about 40% of her sugar was "clayed" or slightly refined before shipping, which gave it a high value on the European market. St. Domingue planters, though inclined to absenteeism like the British, enjoyed low production costs. Their land yielded over 60% more sugar per acre than the most fertile parts of Jamaica.[3] All these advantages had made St. Domingue a potent rival to the British West Indies.

The revolution continued from 1791 to the end of the century. A Negro republic was founded, slaves were returned to work as indentured servants, and agriculture began to revive. But by 1800 St. Domingue had re-established only 21% of her pre-revolutionary volume of sugar exports.[4]

The French island of Guadaloupe, another important exporter of sugar, was struck by revolution and war in 1794. She was still desolate eight years later.[5]

The removal of such a large quantity of produce from the European market had immediate effects. Continental buyers turned to Britain for supplies of sugar and the British West Indian planters, after nearly twenty years of depression, looked forward to famine prices and new markets.[6]

Just at this time new varieties of sugar cane began to appear in the Caribbean from the islands of Bourbon (now Réunion)

[2]Figures prepared by the French Assembly, quoted in Bryan Edwards, *An Historical Survey of the Island of St. Domingo* (London, 1801), 230; and in Ragatz, *Fall of the Planter Class*, 204.
[3]Edwards, *St. Domingo*, 230; Hochstetter, "Wirtschaftlichen and Politischen Motive," 81.
[4]Calculated from *ibid.*, 81, after correlating his figures for 1790–1791 with those of the French Assembly.
[5]Daniel McKinnen, *A Tour Through the British West Indies, in the years 1802 and 1803* (London, 1804), 53.
[6]CO 245:10 contains a well-written "Memoir of St. Domingo" which emphasizes the impact of the revolution on the British economy.

and Tahiti. The Bourbon cane was four times larger than the old variety and yielded about one third more sugar per acre.[7] Its sugar was of a low grade, but continental buyers liked it. Because the new cane could be grown on inferior or partly exhausted soil, it was well suited for expanding production in the older British West Indies.

Unfortunately, British planters were unable to exploit fully the opportunity offered by new canes and open markets. In the first place, adequate credit for expansion was not available. Early in 1793 speculation in war materials brought on a financial collapse in England.[8] Several West Indian merchant and banking firms went bankrupt and planters were unable to obtain large loans for several years after.

Slaves had become more expensive as well. Dolben's Regulating Act caused a reduction in the size of cargoes from Africa just as planters, anticipating abolition, hurried to buy as many slaves as possible. Prices rose almost 30% between 1787 and 1790,[9] reached a peak in 1792, and remained high throughout the war with France.

During that war British Dominica, Grenada, and St. Vincent's suffered revolts by their French minorities. Grenada and St. Vincent's were also plundered by native "Carib" Negroes in 1795. The latter island lost 75% of her sugar crop even though she deported the Caribs and opened their reserved lands to cultivation.[10]

Yet another obstacle to supplying the continental sugar markets was raised by the British government. When the price of muscovado sugar began to jump early in 1792, Pitt told the Society of Planters and Merchants that something must be done to increase the supply in Britain.[11] British consumers, he said, could not be expected to pay famine prices while thousands of tons of sugar were sent to fill continental markets. After several

[7] Ragatz, *Fall of the Planter Class*, 80.
[8] Cf. *HC Sess Pap* 1793(101)XL, "Report on the State of Commercial Credit."
[9] *HC Sess Pap* 1790(698)LXXXVII, 194, 305.
[10] CO 261:9, "Report of the St. Vincent's Legislature," 118 and *passim*.
[11] Min WI Plant, February 20, 1792.

weeks of heated argument with the planters, Pitt drew up a new schedule of tariffs and hurried it through Parliament. The average London price of sugar was to be calculated and published each week in the official *London Gazette*. Whenever it exceeded a stipulated maximum, the whole drawback on re-exported sugar would be withdrawn.[12] Planters and merchants were outspokenly critical. They believed that a period of high prices would be fair compensation for the high costs which they incurred as a result of restrictions on trade with the United States.[13]

Regulation of the drawback on re-exports proved to be both cumbersome and ineffective. Speculators moved in whenever the price of sugar approached the cutoff point. Furthermore, sugar brokers were not averse to forfeiting the drawback if by selling in continental markets they could raise prices in England. The new eagerness for sugar across the Channel made this policy easier. Between 1794 and 1799 the average London price of muscovado far exceeded the 50s. maximum set by Pitt, yet re-exports of sugar reached record levels during the same period.[14]

To keep supplies in the country and to raise revenue for the war, Pitt increased the penalties on sugar exports. By the end of 1799 import duties stood at 20s. per cwt., the drawback at only 11s. The Society of Planters and Merchants objected loudly each time the gap widened, but Pitt refused to compromise.

The policy of tariff restrictions on re-exports, combined with the higher cost of slaves and provisions in the West Indies, kept British planters from fully exploiting the loss of St. Domingue before the end of the century. By that time other colonies, aided by the fortunes of war, had filled the gap and were threatening to ruin the whole European sugar market.

[12] *32 Geo. III, c. 43.* The maximum was set at 60s. per cwt. until July 31, 1792; 55s. from then to October 31, and 50s. thereafter. Similar rules were adopted for the bounty on exports of refined sugar.

[13] For more detailed arguments cf. Min WI Plant, May 10, 1792, and CO 260:11, "Resolutions of a Committee of the Council and Assembly of St. Vincent's held 7 June 1792."

[14] Export figures in *HC Sess Pap* 1807(65)III, 72–73. For a list of wholesale sugar prices, calculated on six-week averages, see below, Appendix I.

Most of the non-British Caribbean colonies which remained in foreign hands throughout the French wars had neither slaves nor capital enough for rapidly expanding their sugar production. But those captured by the British gained immediate access to both, and their produce was admitted to British ports on equal terms with that from the older British colonies. Tobago, Martinique, and the eastern (formerly Spanish) end of St. Domingue were taken from the French in 1794. The Dutch colonies on the coast of South America—Demerara, Surinam, Berbice, and Essequibo—surrendered two years later. Spanish Trinidad was taken in 1797.

Sugar from the captured French islands went immediately onto the British market. Trinidad and the Dutch colonies were far less developed, but both possessed an abundance of fertile land. The latter grew a bright straw-colored sugar highly prized by English grocers, and as soon as British rule was established, many planters from the older West Indies moved to Demerara and Berbice with all their slaves and equipment.[15] Slaves and loans for expansion, which the older colonies had found difficult to obtain, suddenly became plentiful in the new. Thus encouraged, the conquered colonies were able by 1801 to provide 19% of Britain's total imports of sugar.[16]

Meanwhile a few foreign colonies managed to sidestep the difficulties of war and to export sugar to the Continent. Brazil expanded her production rapidly after 1792, and because her Portuguese owners were allies of the British her produce was allowed safe passage across the Atlantic. After reaching Lisbon it was distributed all over the Continent: in 1799, one quarter of all sugar cargoes arriving in Hamburg, the chief depot for such produce, were of Portuguese origin.[17]

A second major exception was Cuba. Lying outside the main theater of naval operations, Cuba was liberally supplied with slaves by British traders. Her muscovado sugar was superior in

---

[15] James Rodway, *History of British Guiana from 1668 to the present* (3 vols., Georgetown, Demerara, 1893), II, 152.
[16] Compare import figures in *HC Sess Pap* 1801–2(55)IV, 289, and 1807(65)III, 72–73.
[17] Min WI Merchants' Society, September 24, 1799.

quality to that of Jamaica and brought 4% to 5% higher prices in European markets. Very little of it was grown before 1790, but by 1805 the estimated amount reaching Europe equalled 70% of St. Domingue's pre-revolutionary exports.[18]

How did the French and Spanish colonial proprietors get their sugar to Europe during the war when British warships controlled the Atlantic routes? Some was shipped in neutral Dutch, Danish, or Swedish vessels,[19] but the amount was never very great. Most went by way of the United States.

By a rule of War laid down in 1756, neutral trade to belligerent territories was restricted to goods normally carried in peacetime. A British Royal Instruction of November 1793 interpreted this Rule to exclude all neutral trade with French colonies, but after violent objections from the United States the Instruction was amended to permit indirect trade to and from Europe.[20] Goods registered as exports of neutral territory in the Americas were allowed to be shipped to British or neutral European ports.

United States merchant shippers soon built up an enormous trade with the French and Spanish colonies. Sugar, rum, and coffee were taken to an American port—imported and exported by a simple exchange of papers—and sent off to Europe under the protection of an American flag.[21] Ships' captains usually listed England as their destination, and might even call there, but only to find out whether London, Le Havre, or Hamburg was the best market.[22]

Despite occasional warnings from Paris and Madrid, French

---

[18] James Stephen, *War in Disguise, or the Frauds of The Neutral Flags* (London, 1805), 230.

[19] Dutch royalists and Scandinavians built a thriving trade in enemy produce by maintaining free ports at a few small, barren West India islands. Cf. James Stephen, *War in Disguise*, 42–43, and Frances Armytage, *Free Ports*, II.

[20] Stephen, *War in Disguise*, 20–23. Cf. Capt. Alfred T. Mahan, *The Influence of Sea Power upon the French Revolution and Empire, 1793–1812* (2 vols., London, 1893), II, 237, 253; and Charles R. King, ed., *The Life and Correspondence of Rufus King* (6 vols., New York, 1894–1900), II, 342.

[21] Mahan, *Sea Power*, II, 268.

[22] J. Stephen, *War in Disguise*, 46.

and Spanish colonists welcomed American merchant shipping throughout the war. They purchased Flemish, German, and Russian manufactures, which were cheaper than the British, and sent their produce to Europe at peacetime rates.[23] As a result of this competitive advantage their agricultural production was greatly stimulated. American re-exports of colonial sugar rose from 213,777 cwt. in 1795 to 788,215 cwt. in 1799, more than the total from all the colonies captured by Britain.[24]

The Caribbean and South American sugar colonies, in fact, were over-compensating for the loss of St. Domingue. Continental markets began to fill up and British factors had difficulty exporting enough sugar to maintain prices at home. If production continued to expand, there would soon be a glut of sugar throughout Europe.

A preview of what was to come occurred in April and May, 1799. European sugar prices were exceptionally high because the available supply from the previous year had been used up and a new crop was not expected until the first of June. In Hamburg, the great sugar depot for northern Europe, speculators were anxiously awaiting the outcome of a diplomatic argument concerning the city's neutrality.[25] Suddenly, over a million cwt. of British sugar, whose re-export had been delayed since December 1798 by foul weather, arrived in the Hamburg market. A general panic ensued. Sugar prices plunged overnight, and some eighty-three merchant firms collapsed.[26]

[23] American shipping and insurance charges were 40% to 45% less than British charges during the war. *Ibid.*, 83. For the wartime trade in colonial supplies, see *HC Sess Pap* 1807(65)III, 55, and Dorothy Burne Goebel, "British Trade to the Spanish Colonies," *American Historical Review*, XLIII, 295–297.

[24] Computed from United States Congress, *American State Papers* (Washington D.C., 1832), VII, papers 31, 38, 42, 47, and 49. For data on the captured colonies, see *HC Sess Pap* 1801–2(55)IV, 289.

[25] Hamburg became the chief European market after ports in the Netherlands were overrun by the French. Her merchants preferred to surrender to the French rather than risk destruction of the city, but England, Prussia, and Russia threatened economic retaliation if they did so. Cf. FO 33:17 and 33:18, letters from Sir James Crawford, British consul in Hamburg, to Grenville.

[26] W. L. Mathieson, *British Slavery and its Abolition, 1823–1838* (London, 1926), 10; Minutes of the Sub-committee of West India Merchants appointed October 3, 1799.

English sugar merchants were hit hard. Re-exports inevitably declined for the rest of the year, whereas imports rose even higher than before. The amount of sugar remaining for sale in Britain was nearly double the average of the previous eight years.[27] Only a sixth of it could be stored in London warehouses.[28] The rest remained in ships' holds, liable to pilfering, damage, and deterioration. Import duties had to be paid even though sugar was difficult to sell, and some merchants lacked sufficient capital to make up the difference.

By October 1, 1799 the sugar depression had spread throughout England and emergency measures were hurriedly taken to avoid disaster. Merchants in Liverpool and Lancaster received Exchequer loans totalling £500,000 with low rates of interest.[29] The London Society of West India Merchants set up a screening committee through which credit might be obtained from the Bank of England.[30] A Bonding and Warehousing Act, passed in October, exempted sugar stored under certain restrictions from all import duties until it was put up for sale. In May 1800 the drawbacks on re-exports of sugar and coffee were temporarily raised and in June permission was given to use sugar in brewing beer. With these several concessions, the British merchants were able not only to avoid bankruptcy, but to hold sugar back from the market until prices returned to normal.[31]

Because the sugar crisis of 1799 was occasioned by a set of unusual circumstances many British sugar merchants tended to regard it as a freak disturbance. In reality, 1799 was only the first of a series of years in which West Indian sugar glutted the British market. Re-exports remained high but imports soared even higher. The amount of sugar left for sale in Britain had averaged 1,446,496 cwt. from 1791 to 1798. During the next

[27] See Appendix II.
[28] Walter M. Stern, "The London Sugar Refiners Around 1800," *Guildhall Miscellany*, number 3, February 1954; Pares, *A West India Fortune*, 196, 200.
[29] Ragatz, *Fall of the Planter Class*, 288.
[30] Minutes of the Subcommittee of West India Merchants appointed October 3, 1799.
[31] Minutes of the West India Merchants' Society, August 15, 1800.

eight years it averaged 2,195,521 cwt.[32] The rapid development of the captured colonies by British investors, using British slaves, was bearing bitter fruit.

Planters in the older British West Indies had been playing a dangerous game. After the upheaval in St. Domingue they had expanded their output of low grade sugar to meet continental demands. This was accomplished, however, by using new varieties of cane on worn-out land along with costly provisions, a method which would have been uneconomic in normal times. Only the prevalence of exceptionally high prices in Europe enabled the planters to make a profit. When slightly better sugar from foreign and captured colonies began to reach the market in larger quantities, and at competitive prices, low grade produce from the older British West Indies became redundant.

The crisis in Britain was relieved for a year by exceptional re-exports of sugar. By the end of 1800 the average wholesale price of muscovado was listed in the *London Gazette* at an all-time high of 78s. per cwt. But in May 1801, reports that a record crop of sugar was on its way from the West Indies caused the market to collapse.[33] Within a few weeks prices fell to an average 55s. per cwt. By June 1802, when the Peace of Amiens was formally ratified, they stood at 34s., the lowest ever recorded.[34]

British merchants had expected that the cessation of hostilities would lead to a prompt revival of continental demand, which would siphon off the overflow from Britain. France, however,

[32]See Appendix II.
[33]The expectation of peace may have been partly responsible for the unprecedented fall in prices. Peace meant increased competition from foreign sugars on the Continent. Expensive but low-grade British sugars would be forced back onto the home market, causing a glut. Significantly perhaps, prices slumped just after the public learned of Lord Hawkesbury's negotiations for peace with France, in May 1801.
[34]See Appendix I. The import duty in 1800 amounted to 20s. per cwt., or 59% by value. Foreign and East Indian sugars, which paid a statutory 34% by value, were thus able to undersell British Caribbean sugar in the British market, an unprecedented situation which horrified the Society of Planters and Merchants.

continued and reinforced her wartime prohibition on all British ships and goods in all the territories she controlled, "in consequence of which," wrote Edward Long, "our West India products still remain a drug upon our hands."[35] Hope of negotiating the opening of French sugar markets was crushed by the renewal of war in July 1803. When French forces occupied Hamburg and Bremen, trade to those cities was shut off by a British blockade. Sugar had to be shipped farther east, mainly to Magdeburg, where less of it could be absorbed.[36]

The renewal of war also brought neutral American and Scandinavian ships back to the non-British colonies. This time, however, they were joined by scores of French merchant vessels which had been secretly transferred to neutral owners on bond for the duration of the war.[37] French and Spanish sugars soon began to flood continental markets, and re-exports from Britain gradually fell off.

The Treaty of Amiens had stipulated the return of the captured colonies (except Trinidad) to their original owners. British planters and merchants had hoped this would at least reduce the influx of sugar into Britain, thereby raising prices again. But before the captured colonies were handed over in the summer of 1802 all their stocks of produce were cleared out and shipped to England.[38] The resulting over-supply of sugar was hardly overcome before war returned and the colonies in question were quickly recaptured.

The short Peace of Amiens had one good result, however. It brought home to British lawmakers the danger of supplying slaves and capital to colonies whose allegiance was temporary and whose development could ruin the older British West Indies.

[35]Robert M. Howard, ed., *Records and Letters of the Family of the Longs of Longville, Jamaica and Hampton Lodge, Surrey* (2 vols., London, 1925), II, 334.
[36]J. Jepson Oddy, *European Commerce, Shewing New and Secure Channels of Trade with the Continent* (London, 1805), 415–416.
[37]Stephen, *War in Disguise*, 9, 71, 97, 114.
[38]Sir William Young, *The West India Commonplace Book* (London, 1807), 61.

Meanwhile, changes had been taking place in the African slave trade which made the effectiveness of a unilateral abolition more certain. Most of the British trade was gradually confined to British colonies, while foreign competitors were virtually eliminated. It was stated that in 1790 British traders supplied about 25,000 slaves each year to foreign colonies.[39] During the first French war this average was reduced nearly 80%.[40] Most of the French and Dutch colonies were either captured or partially destroyed by revolution and war. The Spanish planters at first increased their imports of British slaves despite contrary orders from Madrid, but Pitt cut off this trade entirely in 1797.[41] The captured colonies did not reduce their imports of slaves, of course; the total carried by British traders remained fairly high until 1805. But the change of sovereignty meant that a unilateral abolition of the British slave trade would have greater effect in the Caribbean.

As the British navy increased its control of the Atlantic, non-British slave traders began to disappear. French and Dutch merchant ships were either kept at home to avoid destruction or sent as privateers to harass the British off the coast of Africa. The Spanish never managed to develop a slave trade of their own before they too entered the war. Some of the enemy trade was taken over by United States ships, especially after 1803.[42] But though Liverpool representatives made much of this development, it never became extensive enough to undermine a possible British abolition. Britain's Portuguese allies confined

[39]See pp. 4–5.
[40]Calculated from *HC Sess Pap* 1801–2(88)IV, 476–477. Cf. Armytage, *Free Port System*, 68, who claims that this trade ceased altogether after 1793.
[41]William Cobbett, *The Parliamentary Debates from the year 1803 to the Present Time* (London, reprint by T. C. Hansard, 1812–1820), IV, 1037. Cf. Armytage, *Free Port System*, 4, 70, 101; and Hochstetter, "Wirtschaftlichen und Politischen Motive," 102–103.
[42]Stephen, *War in Disguise*, 75. Non-British colonies were able to expand production despite interruptions in the supply of slaves because their soil was generally more fertile than that in British areas and required less labor per acre to cultivate.

themselves to the supply of their own colonies. They made no attempt to enter foreign slave markets and did not appear likely to do so in the future. Finally, the Danish slave trade was abolished. This event was more important than would appear at first glance. The Danes had used their small, barren West Indian islands as entrepôts for European goods, slaves, and Caribbean produce of all kinds. St. John alone is reported to have passed on 6,000 to 8,000 British slaves every year to other foreign colonies.[43] But since 1792 a Royal Danish Ordinance had regulated imports of slaves with the avowed intention of gradual abolition. On January 1, 1803, the trade was stopped. Britain's pretensions to humanitarian leadership were given a rude rebuff. Within a year she became, ironically, the only European nation still carrying slaves to the Caribbean.

Before that time British West Indian planters, by following a policy of unenlightened self-interest, had alienated many of their supporters in England. By March 1805 the Society of Planters and Merchants considered it necessary to set up a special committee to defend the islands against "the combination which has long aimed to influence the Public Opinion against them."[44] The Society referred not to abolitionists but to champions of the British navigation laws.

Since the 17th century the navigation laws had regulated colonial trade in accordance with the principle that nothing should be purchased outside the Empire that could be supplied from within. After 1783 this principle was applied to the new American states, with the result that British planters had to buy their supplies from British agents. The change was resented in the West Indies because, it was charged, certain supplies were too costly and others impossible, to obtain outside the American states; British shipping was too expensive, slow and uncertain; and rum and molasses, which were formerly exchanged for American supplies, now found no adequate market and re-

---

[43]Hochstetter, "Wirtschaftlichen and Politischen Motive," 70.
[44]Min WI Plant, March 5, 1805.

mained a dead weight on planters' hands.[45] All these objections were overruled in the interests of British merchants and shipowners engaged in the West Indian trade.

The planters, however, refused to accept the decision. During the decade following 1783 their illicit trade with the Americans reached large proportions.[46] Whenever British supplies were late or unavailable, the planters persuaded colonial governors to lift all restrictions for a limited time.[47] Such exceptions often proved damaging to British traders, who would arrive in the West Indies to find markets filled with alien goods. The Privy Council Committee for Trade thought the governors too amenable to planters' arguments and kept up a barrage of instructions and reprovals throughout the years of peace.

When war came, British shipping was so greatly in demand elsewhere that West Indian governors were given greater freedom to suspend the navigation laws. American ships immediately took over most of the provisioning trade, as the comparison below indicates:[48]

Goods Imported by the British West Indies		In British Ships	In U. S. Ships
Corn (bushels)	1793	201,025	40,961
	1794	47,942	365,990
Flour (bushels)	1793	80,497	44,921
	1794	10,432	119,531
Beef and Pork (barrels)	1793	134	6
	1794	0	8,930
Pine Boards (feet)	1793	12,219,298	2,428,426
	1794	1,901,691	7,920,568

[45]*HC Sess Pap* 1784(5)LXV, 3–4. British ships were still allowed to carry American supplies to the West Indies; but this trade too was irregular and slow.
[46]H. C. Bell, "British Commercial Policy in the West Indies," 440.
[47]Cockcroft, *George Chalmers*, 95. For examples, see BT 6:88, 29–30, and CO 101:30, Governor Mathews to Grenville, June 30, 1790.
[48]*HC Sess Pap* 1806(142)XII, 431–433.

It will be noticed that the amount of goods purchased by the West Indians increased generally during the first year of war. Supplies from America did not entirely replace those from Britain, but rather added to the existing trade.[49] However, by 1800 United States ships were carrying 90% of all Anglo-American trade.[50]

The near-monopoly of the provisioning trade by the Americans had three consequences which caused special concern among British ministers of state. First, the Americans began to hold back plantation supplies until prices reached a high level. Then they would sell out their cargoes and proceed to enemy territory for sugar, rum, and coffee. Both policies lowered the competitive value of British colonial produce. Secondly, the American monopoly was believed to be holding back the development of agriculture and forestry in the remaining British colonies of North America. From 1783 to 1793 these colonies, encouraged by the British government, expanded their exports of lumber and provisions to the West Indies. Their merchants claimed they could supply everything the planters needed within a few years if only they were guaranteed a steady market.[51] United States shipping, however, made this impossible. During the war the British North American colonies lost almost all their West Indian trade except the supply of fish from Newfoundland.

The third consequence of American intervention was a break in the traditional compact between West Indian planters and British sugar factors. In July 1799, the London sugar merchants learned that sugar and other colonial produce had been taken from St. Kitt's and Antigua in American vessels in consequence of a shortage of British shipping, and that the Americans were at liberty to proceed to any port they desired.[52] Further en-

---

[49]Cf. *HC Sess Pap* 1807(65)III, 79–80. British exports to the West Indies actually rose 50% or more between 1792 and 1807.

[50]Samuel F. Bemis, *Jay's Treaty: A Study in Commerce and Diplomacy* (New York, 1923), 40. Further data may be found in Sir William Young, *The West India Commonplace Book*, 159.

[51]For an appraisal of the arguments, see BT 6:88, 5, George Rose to Edward Cooke.

[52]Min WI Merchants' Society, July 4, 1799.

quiries convinced the merchants "that from several of the British West India Islands, and more particularly from Jamaica, the Exports of Sugar and Coffee to the United States, and through that medium to Foreign European Ports, is considerable and has of late years been rapidly progressive...."[53] By sending sugar to foreign ports the British planters were defaulting on consignments to England which guaranteed the security of merchants' advances and other West Indian investments. They were also infringing the navigation acts and reducing British shipping and tariff revenues. Such a policy contradicted the whole purpose of the British colonial empire.

Far from apologizing for their actions, the planters continually demanded the reopening of full-scale trade with the United States. They asked Henry Dundas to concede this point during negotiations for Jay's Treaty in 1794, even though the United States had placed an embargo on British trade.[54] They also sent memorials to the Privy Council Committee for Trade, but Lord Liverpool refused even to discuss the issue.[55] On November 21, 1804 the Committee for Trade counterattacked with an Order-in-Council placing severe restrictions on all American commerce with the West Indies, and threatened to dismiss lenient governors.[56] But none of the governors, or their legislatures, was prepared to cooperate on such short notice. They replied that American supplies had become vitally necessary to the survival of the British Caribbean colonies.[57]

The British planters stood condemned for selfish hypocrisy.

[53]*Ibid.*, September 24, 1799. Sir William Young admitted later (*West India Commonplace Book*, 27) that an average 6,000 hogsheads, or 81,000 cwt. of sugar disappeared this way every year between 1794 and 1805. Official import figures in the *American State Papers*, VII, give a much lower average, but some produce may have gone directly to Europe.
[54]Min WI Plant, June 13, 1794.
[55]*Ibid.*, April 30 and May 3, 1804.
[56]During the first war the West Indian governors had been automatically indemnified by act of Parliament for infringing the navigation laws. Now this indemnity was to be given only in cases approved by the Committee for Trade.
[57]Cf. CO111:6, Gov. Beaujon to Camden, May 4, 1805, and BT 6:88, 51–69. Lord Seaforth (Charles Ellis, then Governor of Barbados) tried to enforce the Order-in-Council of 1804 but met with violent opposition from planters and American ships' captains.

When they opposed abolition of the slave trade, or wartime sugar tariffs, or the admission of produce from captured colonies, they cited the "contract" between colonies and mother country based on the navigation laws, which guaranteed their special interests. Yet when they wanted cheap supplies they thought nothing of abandoning that same "contract" at the expense of British merchants, national revenue, and the "nursery for seamen." As a result the planters' reputation in England, especially among those who championed trade for trade's sake, was seriously compromised.

In the Spring of 1804, when concern over the planters' actions was already strong, Parliament was shown the correspondence relating to Charles Ellis's address of 1797. The accumulated bundle of objections, evasions and outright refusals to cooperate with any plan for gradual abolition was deeply incriminating. Confidence in the planters' integrity, which had been such a strong deterrent to moderate abolitionists, sharply diminished.

The planters' economic position had changed considerably between 1788 and 1804. In the former year the value of the West Indies to the British Empire was hardly questioned. They represented a secure source of produce for British consumption or re-export as well as a good market for British manufacturers. Incomes earned in the West Indies were spent either locally or in Britain. Debt was increasing, but it was owed chiefly to British subjects.

By 1804 every one of these conditions had been qualified or even reversed. Produce from the old British West Indies was a drug on the market; its value had been undermined by exports from foreign and captured colonies. The planters' debts had increased rapidly during the short interval of prosperity after 1792 and were now out of all proportion to potential earnings or to assets. Furthermore, some of the produce and revenue which had once gone to British creditors was now being siphoned off illegally by American merchant shippers. In short, the British West Indies were losing the basis for their claim to a privileged position within the imperial economy.

8

The Politics of Abolition

On February 21, 1804 William Wilberforce, writing to his old friend Hannah More, lamented the loss of public enthusiasm for abolition. He had just given notice that a new motion on the subject would be presented to the House of Commons in May, but already there were signs of impending failure. "Alas! The tales of horror, which once caused so many tears to flow, are all forgotten!"[1] It was true. The evidence on slavery and the slave trade was now old and unexciting, the abolitionist organization had disintegrated, and Henry Addington was still in office. There seemed no way out of the doldrums.

To make matters worse, West Indians had suggested a suspension of the slave trade for three or four years in order to frustrate the growth of the captured colonies. Wilberforce would not compromise his own humanitarian principles, but

[1] Wilberforce, *Correspondence of Wilberforce*, I, 299. Wilberforce had written in 1802: "The subject has never been discussed since 1792; since that ere more than half the House of Commons is changed, and a new generation has sprung up in the world. I fear there are very few indeed, who know all the grounds on which the subject rests. They adhere to the party... which they originally joined, and give a languid support, as if by prescription. All the Irish members, to a man, are wholly ignorant on the subject." *Life of Wilberforce*, III, 70–71.

he was certain that Parliament would be more amenable. If the trade were suspended a final decision on abolition would be further delayed.[2]

Before he introduced his bill, however, the situation improved markedly. In a general meeting on May 17 the West Indian body rejected both abolition and suspension of the slave trade. Turning their backs on every form of compromise, they willingly incurred the risk of offending a large section of moderate men in Parliament.

The day following this meeting Addington was forced out of office by the opposition of Fox, Grenville, and Pitt. Grenville refused to return to office without Fox, whom the King resolutely opposed, and Pitt finally accepted the reins of government without his old ally. The new administration was weak,[3] but from an abolitionist point of view it was better than Addington's.

On May 30 Wilberforce asked the House of Commons for leave to bring in his new bill. After a recital of the horrors of Africa, he moved into a new line of attack. Planters' profits, he said, were now down to five or six per cent. In the last twenty years property worth £32 million had been surrendered for debts. Most of the trouble was due to the importation of new slaves, but the planters had done nothing to control these imports or to alleviate the conditions which made them necessary. "Instead of softening and relaxing in their attachment to the system, they seemed to increase in their support of it, and hugged it closer and closer to their bosoms." Also adverting to the wartime economy, he questioned "the expediency of vesting British capital in a part of the dominions of the empire which was most vulnerable, most liable to the external attack of the enemy, and most subject to internal convulsion." Any way it was considered, the slave trade was now a danger to the

[2]Wilberforce, *Correspondence of Wilberforce*, I, 299. The several maneuvers for suspension of the trade are described in the *Life of Wilberforce*, III, 164–167.

[3]George Rose and Charles Long estimated the initial voting strength of the opposition at 270. Harcourt, *Diaries and Correspondence of George Rose*, II, 119.

West Indies. For their sake, if not for the Africans', it should be stopped as soon as possible.[4]

Wilberforce followed up this argument during the committee stage of the bill by presenting the correspondence relating to Ellis's Address in 1797. After reading it, an M. P. who had not spoken on the subject during sixteen years of debate confessed that his last reservations were removed. If any inconvenience now resulted from abolition, it would be the planters' own fault, for they had failed to exert any effort to prepare for the change.[5]

It was Pitt, however, who finished the argument. His speech on June 7, centering on the changes effected by the war, struck at the two strongest pillars of the slave trade defense:

> Now, I appeal to every gentleman in the trade, whether, by the importation of slaves, since the year 1792 to the present time, their property, I mean the original property embarked in this trade, has been improved? Or whether, the whole of the importation since that time has not been for the sake of employing capital in the cultivation of new land in rivalship to the old property in the slave trade? Whether new colonies have not arisen to rival the old ones?
>
> He said, no other nation but England, from its capital, and its hostile and commercial marine, could continue the slave trade; and he concluded with asserting, that this was the most fortunate time at which the humanity of this country could be exercised for the annihilation of the nefarious system. There never before occurred such an opportunity as now offers for the accomplishment of this acknowledged desirable purpose....[6]

The defenders of the slave trade appeared to fall apart when hit by a frontal attack. There were none of the time-worn arguments about planters' integrity or about West Indian trade

---

[4]Cobbett, *Parliamentary Debates*, II, 450–454.
[5]*Ibid.*, 654–655.
[6]*Ibid.*, 551–552.

and investment, none of the smooth confidence of former years. General Tarleton asked only that the principles of morality and religion not be pushed to extremes. William Manning tried to block debate on a technicality, but was ruled out of order. Yet another committee of enquiry was suggested by Addington. In the end, nothing had been said against abolition itself. The House gave Wilberforce leave to bring in his measure by a vote of 124 to 49.[7]

During the remaining stages of the bill the West Indians generally stuck to delaying tactics. They asked for new reports on the Caribbean and African trades, and for additional hearings on London and Liverpool petitions. A compensation clause was demanded.[8] West Indian M. P.'s also absented themselves from committee meetings in order to halt proceedings for lack of a quorum, then attacked Wilberforce for causing delay.[9] Finally, there were persistent attempts to confuse abolition with slave emancipation and to play upon fears of Negro revolt in the Caribbean. None of these maneuvers had any success. The bill passed through all its readings with comfortable majorities.[10]

There its progress ended. Shortly after taking the bill to the House of Lords, Wilberforce was informed by Pitt that the Cabinet had decided to postpone abolition for a year. The Prime Minister added that there was too little time to hear evidence, which the Lords were determined to do, and that if Wilberforce forced a division in the upper House he would certainly lose.[11] There was no choice. On July 3 Lord Hawkesbury, supported by seven of his Cabinet colleagues,[12] formally post-

[7]*Life of Wilberforce*, III, 168. A party of 33 or 34 Irish members organized by Lord De Blaquiere, a leader in Irish politics since 1772, held a dinner in honor of Wilberforce and then voted for him as a group.

[8]Cf. Cobbett, *Parl. Deb.*, II, 662–663. Pitt rejected a discussion of compensation on the ground that it involved a public expense which had not been recommended in the King's Speech at the beginning of the session.

[9]*Life of Wilberforce*, III, 176.

[10]Cobbett, *Parl. Deb.*, II, 546, 552, 662, 848, 871.

[11]*Life of Wilberforce*, III, 180–181.

[12]Pitt was the only Commons man in this Cabinet.

THE POLITICS OF ABOLITION 129

poned debate to the next session. Said Wilberforce, "I was never so dissatisfied with Pitt as this time."[13]

The long-standing friendship between the two men was not strengthened during the course of the year. Pitt, struggling to overcome the discordant elements in his administration, had little time for Wilberforce's inconvenient crusade. After Addington (now Viscount Sidmouth) entered the Cabinet in January 1805, agreement on policy became even harder. In these circumstances Pitt wished to avoid a controversy over abolition, and in February 1805 he asked Wilberforce once again to postpone his bill to some more propitious time.[14] Wilberforce refused.

The new abolition bill was resolutely attacked by the West India Planters and Merchants. On February 14 their Standing Committee approved resolutions deploring any discussion of the question while the colonies were threatened by Negro revolts, and sent copies to every M. P. the following day. A special committee of thirty-five, including most of the West Indians in Parliament, was given power to organize a "firm and vigorous opposition." Tribute was paid to the Duke of Clarence, who had attended the meeting to offer his full support.[15] A week later Edmund P. Lyon, the agent for Jamaica, received a blank check "for any expenses he may be subjected to in conducting the opposition to the abolition of the slave trade."[16]

By the time the bill was given its first reading on February 19 support was already dwindling. The Irish, who had voted as a group for abolition the previous year, had since been converted by West Indian arguments. Those who did not oppose Wilberforce this time simply stayed away from the House. Some Scots M. P.'s, formerly neutral, also joined the opposition.[17]

[13] *Life of Wilberforce*, III, 178.
[14] *Ibid.*, 211.
[15] Min WI Plant, February 4, 1805. Wilberforce noted in his diary, "Great canvassing of our enemies."
[16] Min WI Plant, February 25, 1805.
[17] *Life of Wilberforce*, III, 177, 212.

The debate on the second reading of the bill was painfully one-sided. The Liverpool members found courage to speak again after several years of silence. They were supported by Sir William Young and three other West Indians, and by Lord Sidmouth's brother and spokesman, Hiley Addington. Wilberforce and Fox stood almost alone; Pitt remained silent. The bill was defeated by seven votes, and Wilberforce noted that "many persons excuse themselves for not voting with me on the ground of Pitt's not meaning it to be carried."[18]

Pitt's sincerity in the matter of abolition has always been subject to doubt. But the charge that he sacrificed humanitarian principles in order to maintain his political position is perhaps too narrowly conceived. For Wilberforce also had a degree of political influence based on his leadership of the group of evangelical reformers known as the "Clapham Sect" and on his representation of Yorkshire, the largest constituency in England. It appears that before 1805 he gave this influence unreservedly to Pitt, expecting that the Prime Minister would do his best to arrange a political atmosphere friendly or at least neutral toward the progress of abolition. By implicitly delegating such authority, Wilberforce was left free to cultivate his moral leadership, and until the Spring of 1805 he continued to believe in the efficacy of that arrangement.[19] After Pitt's apparent desertion, however, he decided to make better use of his political influence. And for once he wisely aimed at a specific, limited objective.

The colonies captured during the wars with France had never received constitutional self-government. Consequently their

[18]*Ibid.*, 216. Wilberforce doubted the truth of this excuse, but it might explain why Lord De Blaquiere, a loyal Pittite, was unable to rally the Irish for abolition again.

[19]For example, Wilberforce wrote to Lord Grenville in June 1804, "Though I have been so long in parliament, I was ignorant till yesterday evening, when I accidentally learned it ... that in the House of Lords a bill from the House of Commons is in a destitute and orphan state, unless it has some peer to adopt and take the conduct of it." (*Life of Wilberforce*, III, 179). Grenville himself had done this work in the 1790's; and in 1804 it was he who solicited the help of Lord Harrowby, the Foreign Secretary, as sponsor to the abolition bill.

slave trade could still be regulated or even prohibited by an Order-in-Council. Wilberforce had been seeking such an Order since 1797 but was always put off on one pretext or another.[20] Now on March 9, 1805 he informed Pitt that if the government would not act, he himself would bring in a bill for the partial abolition, and he threatened to join the opposition parties to obtain support. To make clear his determination, Wilberforce held a meeting with Fox, Henry Petty, Charles Grey, and other Foxites to discuss possible legislative action. Pitt's Cabinet was more frightened of a parliamentary conflict in March than it had been in February, and so Wilberforce was promised an Order-in-Council in the near future.[21]

During the next four months two principal opponents of abolition were removed from office. Lord Melville (Henry Dundas) was censored by the Commons for permitting irregularities in Admiralty Office finance. He was replaced by Charles Middleton, Lord Barham, a staunch abolitionist.[22] Near the end of June Lord Sidmouth and his ally Buckinghamshire, feeling isolated and increasingly neglected, also resigned. The way was now clear for an Order-in-Council, and Pitt, badly in need of political support, hastened to comply with Wilberforce's demand.

It is doubtful that the need to placate abolitionists was felt so strongly by other members of the Cabinet. But a reduction of the slave trade to the captured colonies was by this time vital for the preservation of the old British West Indies' econ-

[20]An Order prohibiting the slave trade to the captured colonies was actually prepared in November 1804, but was not presented to the Privy Council, partly because its form was incorrect and partly, it seems, because Pitt or Wilberforce thought the threat from rival sugar colonies would help secure an act for total abolition in 1805. Wilberforce, *Correspondence of Wilberforce*, I, 341, and *Life of Wilberforce*, III, 184.

[21]Wilberforce, *Correspondence of Wilberforce*, II, 14–15; *Life of Wilberforce*, III, 216, 217, 233. The Order-in-Council was to have been issued by the Colonial Secretary, Lord Camden, on May 12; but his version was so wretchedly drafted that Wilberforce prevented its publication, until extensive revisions could be made. *Ibid.*, 230.

[22]"A superannuated Methodist ... to catch the votes of Wilberforce and Co. now and then." Thomas Creevey, quoted in Ziegler, *Addington*, 238.

omy. Accordingly Lord Eldon and Lord Castlereagh, both former opponents of Wilberforce, cooperated in preparing the Order-in-Council.[23] Issued on August 15, 1805, the Order generally prohibited imports of slaves into the colonies captured since 1802. Exceptions might be made if natural causes seriously reduced the local laboring force, but on no account were the yearly imports to exceed three per cent of the existing slave population in each colony.[24]

Significantly, the Order attracted little notice from defenders of the slave trade. Wilberforce had been correct in assuming that "the West Indians themselves (the old islands I mean) have always been the strongest advocates for stopping the importation of slaves into Dutch Guiana..."[25] By the same logic, a bill to abolish the trade to foreign colonies would now have a good chance of success. Lord Henry Petty would have introduced such a measure in 1805 had he not been raised to the peerage upon the death of his father, Lord Lansdowne.[26]

Wilberforce's satisfaction at his partial success was soon qualified by the loss of the prime minister. On January 23, 1806 Pitt died, worn out by overwork and disheartened by the war. It is doubtful that he could have carried the final abolition, for his political weakness was extreme. And it is sad to reflect that only through his demise was Wilberforce given access to the power to complete his grand design.

The new administration was formed by Fox, Grenville, and Sidmouth. They were strange bedfellows, and there were many arguments over patronage and prestige. But Fox proved an able administrator and charmed his way into friendship with George III, while Sidmouth, by deserting his conservative allies for a

---

[23]Castlereagh, then Colonial Secretary, initiated the Order and the instructions to governors involved. Eldon approved their legal form but inserted a contract clause, exempting slave ships already under way to the captured colonies, which Wilberforce considered "utterly detestable." Wilberforce, *Correspondence of Wilberforce*, II, 33–34. The preamble of the Order stressed economic motives so that anti-abolitionist ministers could support it without embarrassment. *Life of Wilberforce*, III, 231.

[24]*HC Sess Pap* 1806(124)I, 289. The Order is also printed, with instructions to governors, in the Privy Council Register, PC 2:168, 227.

[25]Wilberforce, *Correspondence of Wilberforce*, I, 239.

[26]*Life of Wilberforce*, III, 260.

place in the Whig ministry, suffered a political decline.[27] After a few months in office, therefore, Fox and Grenville felt strong enough to initiate a semi-official bill for abolition.[28] After discussing all possible compromises they decided on a measure confirming the Order-in-Council of 1805 and extending its provisions to foreign colonies. Total abolition would follow if all went well.

The bill was introduced on March 31, 1806 by Attorney General Sir Arthur Piggot, a neutral figure who, it was hoped, would dispel the personal animosity usually directed against Wilberforce. The first reading was unopposed, and to the abolitionists' relief the West Indian M. P.'s remained silent. The Society of Planters and Merchants, in fact, had resolved to "pay strict attention" to the bill and to fight "any of the provisions thereof, which may tend to the prejudice of the interests of the British West India Colonies." But they did not challenge its general purpose.[29] In the House, Sir William Young "approved of the principle of the bill, which he considered a boon to the West India merchants, and stated that he had been at a numerous meeting of London merchants, where a majority had agreed with him."[30]

As in 1788, the defense of the trade was left to the Liverpool representatives and to champions of trade in any form like George Rose. They failed, as they had in 1788, to make any impact on the House. The partial abolition bill was given its second and third readings without a division.[31]

The subsequent proceedings in the upper House were managed very skillfully by William Eden, Lord Auckland. Though

[27]In July 1805 Fox estimated Addington's strength at sixty votes, but in December 1806 Charles Long gave him only thirty. The election that month cost him another sixteen to eighteen votes. Pares, *George III and the Politicians*, 79, note 3.
[28]It could not be made a Cabinet measure because Sidmouth was opposed, but Fox and Grenville made it clear to Parliament that they supported the bill as ministers of the Crown, not just as individuals. Cf. Cobbett, *Parl. Deb.*, VII, 508.
[29]Min WI Plant, April 11, 1806.
[30]Cobbett, *Parl. Deb.*, VI, 805. I have found no record of this meeting in the archives of the West India Committee.
[31]*Ibid.*, VI, 805, 919. The bill as amended in committee is in *HC Sess Pap* 1806(124)I, 289–301.

the King was disinclined to interfere, six of his sons threw their weight against abolition,[32] and Lord Hawkesbury was still determined to preserve every aspect of England's trade. Auckland, however, managed to postpone the main discussion until the third reading of the bill while Grenville quietly rounded up support. Then, with the surprising adherence of Sidmouth, Buckinghamshire, and Ellenborough,[33] the abolitionist ministers carried the final division 43 to 18.

The decision of the upper House was not so much a reversal as a logical consequence of its former hostility to abolition. Many peers had based their opposition on the need to preserve British West Indian agricultural production. For that same reason they were compelled to discourage the development of rival colonies by cutting off their supply of new slaves. On the other hand, there was not much that the Lords or the Commons could do after the Order-in-Council of August 15, 1805 had been issued. Like the Order of 1783 which restricted United States-West Indian commerce,[34] the Order of 1805 could have been renewed and the slave trade to the captured colonies proscribed for several years without the sanction of Parliament.

The new act (46 Geo. III, c. 52) prevented British merchants from trading in slaves under a foreign flag, and prohibited the fitting out of foreign ships in British ports, a practice long favored by U. S. merchants. The main effect, however, was to destroy three-quarters of the British slave trade.[35] That which remained did not benefit the sugar planters, who were now too

[32]The Dukes of York, Clarence, Cumberland, Kent, Sussex and Cambridge (Romilly, *Memoirs*, I, 146). The Prince of Wales had promised Fox "not to stir adversely" and his principal advisor, Lord Moira, supported the bill. *Life of Wilberforce*, III, 259. For the King's condition at this time, cf. Pares, *George III and the Politicians*, 156, 184.

[33]Cobbett, *Parl. Deb.*, VII, 34 and 230–231. Ellenborough (Edward Law) had been counsel for the Society of Planters and Merchants in 1792.

[34]Cf. H. C. Bell, "British Commercial Policy in the West Indies," 435 ff.

[35]The available figures are open to some doubt. Picton (*Memorials of Liverpool*, I, 277), says foreign colonies took 13,800 slaves in 1804; while according to HC Sess Pap 1806(265)XIII the conquered colonies, except Trinidad, took about 13,000 between October 1804 and October 1805. Trinidad and the old British West Indies received 8,000 in the same period, or less than one quarter of the total.

impoverished to afford new slaves. Most of it went to a new group of coffee growers in Jamaica whose crops were intended for the continental market.[36] To many members of Parliament, therefore, it seemed a good time to complete the abolition of the slave trade.

The Society of Planters and Merchants thought differently. They expected a future revival of West Indian prosperity and clung to the belief that new imports of slaves would be necessary to sustain agricultural production. When they heard early in June 1806 that Fox was to introduce a measure for total abolition, they quickly mounted a fresh campaign of opposition. Statements condemning further legislation were advertised for two weeks in all the morning newspapers. A subcommittee was appointed to collect the long-overdue levy on "trade", and £500 was voted for use in counteracting the efforts of abolitionist pamphleteers.[37]

But Fox took his opponents by surprise. Instead of a bill, which might have been delayed until the end of the session, he introduced a resolution calling on Parliament to take "effectual measures" for total abolition during the following session "in such manner, and at such period, as may be deemed advisable."[38] Only one vote was required and the abolitionists won it, 114 to 15.[39] The House of Lords gave its consent two weeks later, on June 25. Opposition to the resolution had been partially disarmed by the elimination of the foreign slave trade, and because the session was nearly at an end only the most intransigent defenders of the slave trade attended the debates. The abolitionist ministers took care to preserve a sufficient majority until the day appointed for voting.

[36]*HC Sess Pap* 1806(265)XIII, 801; and *HC Sess Pap* 1805(39)X, 655–657, Report of the Jamaica Assembly.
[37]Min WI Plant, June 9, 1806.
[38]*House of Commons Journals*, June 10, 1806.
[39]*Ibid*. The timing of the resolution is interesting. The House was then considering a bill to legalize open trade between the U. S. and the West Indies, a measure which temporarily disrupted the planter-merchant shipper alliance, and which may account for the small vote cast against abolition. On the other hand Fox wanted to secure the resolution before illness forced him to retire, which happened on June 13.

Fox's resolution was followed with an Address asking the King to seek negotiations with foreign powers for an international agreement to end the slave trade. In order to prevent a last-minute rush for slaves, Parliament also passed a bill limiting the African trade to ships already engaged in it. Now the only question was whether Fox and Grenville could stay in office long enough to complete their design. The opposition groups, led by Lord Hawkesbury and the Duke of Cumberland, were making desperate attempts to dislodge them.

Fox died in September 1806. Most of his adherents accepted the leadership of Charles Grey and continued to cooperate with Grenville. But the strength of the government was compromised by a House of Commons whose members had been elected in 1802 under conditions no longer prevailing. Grenville therefore felt justified in calling for an election in December 1806 and in using every device known to politicians at that time to ensure the return of a favorable majority.[40] The new Parliament proved better than expected: "from 430 to 500 friends, from 120 to 130 contrary, and the rest doubtful or absent."[41]

Meanwhile, Grenville tried to decide how best to revive the subject of abolition. He had been so unsure of his position in June 1806 that he had offered to compromise with Lord Sidmouth on a measure for gradual abolition. His scheme, based on a progressive tax on imported slaves, would not have pleased Wilberforce, and from the way in which Grenville carefully calculated the balance of misery involved one wonders what kind of an abolitionist he really was.[42] Fortunately for his reputation the compromise was forgotten. The results of the December election made an immediate prohibition of the slave trade appear more practicable.

In order to capitalize on the impact of his victory, Grenville initiated the abolition bill in the House of Lords soon after the election. Throughout the month of January 1807 he pushed it relentlessly through the various stages, brushing off attempts

[40]*Dropmore MSS*, VIII, introduction, xlvi.
[41]*Ibid.*, 456.
[42]*Ibid.*, 169. The "tax" plan was first suggested in 1789. See above p. 79.

THE POLITICS OF ABOLITION   137

by Hawkesbury and the Earl of Westmoreland to force another protracted enquiry.[43] Counsel for the petitioners of Liverpool and Jamaica were allowed to speak on February 2. But when they asked permission to call witnesses, to show once more the amount of capital and revenue concerned with the slave trade, Grenville cut them off. This bill would be nonsense, he said, if the property and persons of British subjects were not involved. That was what abolition was all about.[44]

The debate closed on February 5 with an impressive tribute to the memory of Fox by his nephew, Lord Holland.[45] There had been extensive canvassing of votes by both sides, but the abolitionists won the vital second reading by a margin of 100 to 36. Although the bill was amended in committee, no further divisions were recorded. On February 10 the measure was passed to the House of Commons.

The reasons for victory in the House of Lords are not clear. Undoubtedly some peers felt less protective toward proprietors of the older West Indies after the latter had supported the partial abolition of 1806. Perhaps it seemed futile to defend a slave trade already reduced to a quarter of its former size. But these factors were negative and do not fully account for the size of Grenville's majority. The strength of the minister's political position, his command of patronage and promotions within the peerage, and his long experience as Leader of the House must all have contributed to his success. Finally, credit must be given for sheer hard work, for Grenville spent an impressive amount of time enlisting the support of lukewarm or unpredictable peers.

Grenville's decision to initiate the bill in the upper House was undoubtedly wise. Once that stubborn wall was breached, an army of enthusiasts rushed in to fight. "Astonishing eager-

[43]Cobbett, *Parl. Deb.*, VIII, 257–259, 431–432, 601.
[44]*Ibid.*, VIII, 613.
[45]"Everyone agrees in Ld. Holland's speech being fine for anybody, and much the best he ever made, the part about his Uncle very affecting." Castilia Countess Granville, ed., *Lord Granville Leveson Gower: Private Correspondence, 1781–1821* (2 vols., London, 1916), II, 238; Lady Bessborough to Lord Gower.

ness of House," noted Wilberforce; "six or eight starting up to speak at once, young noblemen etc. and asserting high principles of rectitude."[46] Two hundred eighty-three of them voted for the second reading of the bill against sixteen opponents. The abolition bill, having been amended in the Commons, required another passage through the Lords, and by a series of errors in drafting new clauses it was held up until March 25. On that day Grenville went out of office, forced to resign after a monumental misunderstanding with the King on the issue of Catholic Emancipation. It has been suggested that had the new ministry come into office a day earlier abolition would have failed.[47] Yet as early as March 21 Wilberforce was informed that since Parliament's feelings were no longer in question Lords Eldon, Hawkesbury, and Castlereagh "declare that now they will lend themselves to anything needful to effect the measure."[48]

A minority of West Indians, chiefly those still resident in the islands, resisted abolition to the last. In October 1807 the Jamaica House of Assembly published a series of resolutions claiming for itself the sole right of legislating for the colony and declaring "that it is their duty, by all constitutional means, to resist the attempt that has been, and every attempt that may be made, to destroy or abridge that right." The abolition of the slave trade was, among other things,

> subversive of an antient and admitted principle of the British Constitution, that no laws can be binding on those who are not represented in the Parliament which enacts them; placing not only our rights and properties, but also our lives, in the most imminent danger, and tending to promote disaffection in the minds of his Majesty's most loyal subjects.[49]

[46]*Life of Wilberforce*, III, 295.
[47]G. M. Trevelyan, *Lord Grey of the Reform Bill*, 158.
[48]*Life of Wilberforce*, III, 301.
[49]*Gentleman's Magazine*, 1808, 76. "Resolutions of the Jamaica House of Assembly."

The Jamaicans even threatened to cut off supplies to the British troops on the island. But nothing ever happened. In 1807 the West Indies were in no position to browbeat the Parliament of Great Britain. The time for ringing declarations was over, and the time for coming to grips with the social and economic heritage of slavery itself had already arrived.

# 9

Conclusion

The central issue in Parliament's long discussion of the slave trade was whether its abolition could be achieved without seriously damaging British West Indian agriculture and commerce. That issue was complicated by the willingness of other European colonial powers to monopolize the slave trade for the development of their own tropical possessions. The terms of the debate in England were set not by abolitionists but by their opponents, chiefly the West Indian planters. Wilberforce's characterization of the slave trade as a national sin, which must be eliminated immediately at any cost, was not accepted by the majority of Parliament.

Both sides acknowledged that the slave trade was made necessary by the high rate of mortality among slaves in the West Indies, and neither side believed the mortality could be significantly reduced under existing conditions. Planters asserted that amelioration of the slaves' condition had progressed as far as the security of the white population allowed. Wilberforce, on the other hand, argued that abolishing the trade in human beings would force planters to treat their existing slaves better, in order to increase the rate of population growth by natural means.

CONCLUSION   141

A majority in Parliament refused to accept the extreme views of either of the contending parties. Gradual abolition, however, predicated on specific improvements in West Indian slave conditions, and guaranteed by a fixed date for prohibition, found abundant support whenever it was suggested. Henry Dundas's gradualist plan of 1792 was approved by a large majority in the House of Commons despite opposition from both extremes. Similar proposals were considered as late as 1806.

Parliament's preference for gradual abolition should not be condemned either as a manifestation of capitalist greed or as a hypocritical evasion of moral responsibility. The fact was, no one could be sure of the effects of abolition on the West Indian economy until, perhaps, after the Peace of Amiens. The gradualist members of Parliament were simply adopting a program to help the slaves that would not at the same time undermine the imperial economy. After all, Dundas's proposals of 1792 had envisaged a program of cooperation between the British government and the West Indian legislatures, leading to a complete but financially non-destructive abolition by 1800, seven years before the actual event. The slave trade to foreign colonies would have ended in 1793 instead of 1806, and the development of the captured colonies might never have become an issue. Finally, a law based on Dundas's proposals need not have been any less effective than the abolition of 1807, because the cut-off date was not dependent upon the planters' cooperation. If slaveowners had not prepared for the end of the slave trade by 1800, that would have been their own misfortune.[1]

Both Wilberforce and his opponents, however, frustrated the gradualist intentions of the majority in Parliament. By insisting

[1] At the end of the Pitt papers on the slave trade (PRO 30/8:310) is an anonymous memorandum proposing gradual abolition which is strikingly similar to Dundas's proposals. The author concluded, after outlining his plan, that "if its success should be prevented in certain instances by the perversity of the planters, such proprietors after the experience of a few years would be deservedly punished by the abolition of the Negro Trade." I believe this memorandum to be the Dundas proposal of 1796 which prompted Charles Ellis to initiate his address to the King the following year.

on an early date for abolition regardless of the planters' readiness to accept it, Wilberforce antagonized Dundas and alienated the political support which might have accelerated a decision in the House of Lords. His stubbornness offended many would-be abolitionists and contributed to the series of defeats he suffered between 1792 and 1800. Conversely, Wilberforce's withdrawal from leadership in the parliamentary debates of 1806 and 1807 smoothed the final path to success.

For the planters, refusal to accept the principle of gradual abolition, even when put forth by their own parliamentary spokesmen, brought a loss of gradualist support in the fight against immediate abolition. By securing, in 1806, a privileged position in both the North American and African trades at the expense of their former allies, they dissipated the remainder of their original parliamentary influence in the question of the slave trade.

The West Indian case against abolition was undercut by several economic and political developments hitherto largely neglected by historians of the anti-slavery movement. A study of these developments shows that Wilberforce's crusade, though vitally necessary to the success of abolition, was not sufficient to achieve that success in itself. Parliament might not have adopted the abolitionist solution to the problem of West Indian overproduction, had the idea not been so well publicized. Yet the evidence suggests that over-production, and not the evils of slavery and the slave trade, was the more powerful incentive for Parliament's action.

Political considerations also had as much to do with the success or failure of the several abolition bills as Wilberforce's humanitarian crusade. The Regulating Act of 1788 was initiated in Wilberforce's absence by a few individuals on the fringe of the abolitionist organization. Its final form was largely the work of Lord Hawkesbury, who piloted it through the House of Lords without any discernable moral fervor, and it passed only after the Prime Minister had made it a Cabinet issue.

Pitt's political position affected abolition's subsequent fortunes. After 1793, he agreed to moderate his support of the movement in return for the adherence of the Portland Whigs.

CONCLUSION 143

In 1799 his attempt at compromise was wrecked by the intransigence of Portland, Hawkesbury, and other ministers. After Addington joined Pitt's second ministry in January 1805, and tensions were building within the Cabinet, Pitt discouraged Wilberforce's new initiative. Later that same year he agreed to prohibit part of the slave trade because Wilberforce's cooperation was necessary to the government's survival and because economic considerations had neutralized the anti-abolitionists in the Cabinet.

In many accounts of abolition, Charles James Fox is given credit for securing the decisive legislation. Yet his Foreign and Captured Colonies Slave Trade Bill of 1806 was but a confirmation of Pitt's earlier Order-in-Council. The resolution Fox proposed in July 1806, promising action on the slave trade, was no more binding than were the resolutions of 1788 or 1792. The more effective side of the Ministry of All-the-Talents was represented by Lord Grenville. It was he who piloted the 1806 bill through the House of Lords, with the help of his ally Lord Auckland. And he alone engineered the final victory of abolition in 1807.

In sum, the abolition of the British slave trade was made possible by the brief conjunction of a set of economic conditions necessitating restrictions on the productive capacity of the British Caribbean colonies, an unprecedented control of the slave trade itself by British subjects, and a strong, abolition-minded ministry. When one considers the unusual origins of these three factors, and the governmental influence enjoyed by the younger Hawkesbury and other anti-abolitionists after March 1807, one must conclude that the prohibition of the British slave trade was an essentially fortuitous achievement.

APPENDIX I

AVERAGE PRICES OF MUSCOVADO (BROWN) SUGAR, EXCLUSIVE OF ALL CUSTOMS DUTIES, FOR SIX-WEEK PERIODS[1]

Six Weeks Preceding		Ave. s.	Price d.	Six Weeks Preceding		Ave. s.	Price d.
20 Feb.	1793	56	2¾	5 Jan.	1800	57	6¼
19 June	"	59	9	5 April	"	66	2
24 Aug.	"	58	10¼	10 Nov.	"	71	3½
23 Oct.	"	51	10	10 May	1801	48	2½
22 Feb.	1794	51	9¼	20 June	"	53	6
21 June	"	40	2	10 Aug.	"	50	11¼
15 Oct.	"	38	4¾	9 Nov.	"	47	8¾
18 Feb.	1795	48	3¼	10 May	1802	38	8
17 June	"	55	6¾	10 Aug.	"	37	4
22 Aug.	"	60	7½	10 Nov.	"	34	5
23 Oct.	"	60	7¼	5 Jan.	1803	34	4
23 Feb.	1796	63	8½	5 May	"	39	2¼
23 Oct.	1796	62	7½	5 Sept.	"	46	6¼
23 Feb.	1797	64	7	5 Jan.	1804	43	6¼
23 Aug.	"	64	10	5 May	"	49	10
23 Oct.	"	62	11¾	5 Sept.	"	54	3½
23 Feb.	1798	67	3½	5 Jan.	1805	55	1¾
23 June	"	68	11¾	5 May	"	52	8¼
23 Aug.	"	65	11	5 Sept.	"	51	8½
23 Oct.	"	67	6¼	5 Jan.	1806	48	6¾
23 Feb.	1799	69	3¼				

[June-Oct. prices unstable and very low.]

[1806–1807 average: 38s.]

[1]From *HC Sess Pap* 1806(142)XII, 315.

APPENDIX II

AMOUNT OF SUGAR RETAINED FOR CONSUMPTION IN GREAT BRITAIN, 1791–1806: TOTAL IMPORTS MINUS TOTAL RE-EXPORTS

Note: Figures for imports and exports vary from source to source. Two lists are given here for comparison.

Year	Retained (cwt.)[1]	Retained (cwt.)[2]
1791	1,403,211	
1792	1,361,593	
1793	1,677,097	1,939,640
1794	1,489,394	1,857,701
1795	1,336,340	1,709,508
1796	1,554,061	1,840,307
1797	1,273,723	1,606,957
1798	1,476,552	1,825,039
1799	2,772,437	3,097,970
1800	1,506,922	2,156,196
1801	2,319,002	3,198,315
1802	2,250,311	2,923,669
1803	1,693,284	2,087,795
1804	2,144,369	2,670,008
1805	2,076,103	2,555,017
1806	2,801,740	3,290,307

[1] *HC Sess Pap* 1807(65)III, 72–73.
[2] *HC Sess Pap* 1847–8(400)LVIII, 527.

BIBLIOGRAPHY

Manuscript Sources

Bristol University Library, Pinney Papers
British Museum, Additional Manuscripts:
- 12404 Edward Long's *History of Jamaica* with MS notes for a revised version.
- 12431 Papers of Edward Long, 1784–1799.
- 12432 Long papers on Jamaica; minutes of the Jamaica Assembly of 1792 dealing with the slave trade.
- 12433 Speech of Edward Law, counsel for the Society of Planters and Merchants, May 14, 1792.
- 12439 An anti-abolition tract in the Long papers.
- 22900 Correspondence of George Chalmers, 1787–1792.
- 22901 Correspondence of George Chalmers, 1792–1807.
- 38191, 38192, 38194 Letters to the first Lord Liverpool, 1778–1808.
- 38223 Official correspondence of Lord Liverpool
- 38391 Minutes of the Privy Council Committee for Trade, 1788–1789.
- 38416 Liverpool papers from the Privy Council Committee for Trade enquiry on the slave trade, 1788–1789.
- 51469 Charles James Fox, general correspondence, 1806.

Public Record Office Papers:
- B 1:105 — Register of cases in the Court of Bankruptcy, 1803–1806.
- BT 3:1–2 — Board of Trade out-letters, 1787–1789, including enquiries on the slave trade.
- BT 6:9–11 — Copies of evidence used in the Privy Council Committee report on the slave trade, 1789.
- BT 6:70 — Correspondence relating to the transporting of Chinese to Trinidad, 1801–1807.
- BT 6:75 — Correspondence relating to Jamaica.
- BT 6:88 — United States-West Indian commerce reports.
- BT 6:185 — West Indian trade statistics, 1697–1802.
- BT 6:188 — Trade reports, West Indies and America, 1784–1801.
- BT 6:189 — West Indian shipping accounts, 1786–1791.

BIBLIOGRAPHY

BT 6:235	Jamaica trade statistics, 1798–1801.
CO 28:61	Correspondence with Barbados, 1786–1788.
CO 28:73	Correspondence with Barbados, 1805.
CO 31:43	Official papers from Barbados, 1800–1803.
CO 101:30	Papers from Grenada, 1790.
CO 111:6	Correspondence with Demerara and Essequibo, 1805–1806.
CO 112:4	Official despatches to Demerara and Essequibo.
CO 152:65	Correspondence relating to the Leeward Islands, 1786–1788.
CO 152:76	Official correspondence with the Leeward Islands, 1794–1796.
CO 152:78	Minutes of the General Assembly of the Leeward Islands, containing Sir William Young's letters on Ellis's address of 1797.
CO 245:10	Observations on St. Domingue, ca. 1795, in French with an English precis.
CO 260:11	Remonstrance against abolition from St. Vincent's, 1790–1792.
CO 261:9	Letter book of Sir William Young, 1794–1802.
CO 295:11	Despatches from the governor of Trinidad, 1805–1806.
CO 296:1–2	Precis of correspondence with Trinidad, 1797–1807.
CO 296:4	Letters from the Secretary of State to Trinidad, 1801–1810.
CO 324:120–1	Miscellaneous letters from the Secretary of State, 1805, containing the Order-in-Council prohibiting the slave trade to conquered colonies.
FO 33:17	Reports from the British consul in Hamburg, ca. 1799.
FO 33:18	Correspondence with the British consul in Hamburg.
PC 2:168	Privy Council Register, October-November 1805, containing Order-in-Council prohibiting the slave trade to the conquered colonies.
PRO 30/8:101, 104, 121, 154, 193	Correspondence of William Pitt.
PRO 30/8:310	Pitt papers on the slave trade.

PRO 30/8:350 Pitt papers on Demerara and Trinidad
PRO 30/8:363 Pitt papers on Africa and Sierra Leone.

West India Committee Archives, London:
"Minutes of the Society of West India Merchants of London".
"Minutes of the Sub-committee of West India Merchants appointed October, 1799".
"Minutes of the Society of West India Planters and Merchants of London".

Society of Merchant Venturers Archives, Bristol:
"Minutes of the New West India Society".
"Proceedings of the Society of Merchant Venturers of Bristol".

Published Works

Akinjogbin, I. A., "Archibald Dalzel: Slave Trader and Historian of Dahomey," in *Journal of African History*, vol. VII, part I (1966), 67–78.
Allen, W. Gore, *King William IV*. London, 1960.
Armytage, Frances, *The Free Port System in the British West Indies; a study in commercial policy, 1766–1822*. London, 1953.
Aspinall, Arthur, ed., *The Correspondence of George, Prince of Wales, 1770–1812*. 3 vols., London, 1963–65.
———, ed., *The Later Correspondence of George III*. 5 vols., Cambridge, 1963–66.
———, "The Reporting and Publishing of the House of Commons Debates, 1771–1834," in R. Pares and A. J. P. Taylor, eds., *Essays Presented to Sir Lewis Namier*. London, 1956.
Baines, Thomas, *History of the Commerce and Town of Liverpool*. London, 1852.
Bagot, Captain Josceline, ed., *George Canning and his Friends*. 2 vols., London, 1919.
Barnes, Donald Grove, *George III and William Pitt, 1783–1806*. Stanford, 1939.
Bass, Robert D., *The Green Dragoon: The Lives of Banastre Tarleton and Mary Robinson*. London, 1957.
Bath and Wells, Bishop of, ed., *The Journals and Correspondence of William, Lord Auckland*. 4 vols., London, 1861.
Bell, Herbert C., "British Commercial Policy in the West Indies, 1783–1793," *English Historical Review*, XXXI (July 1916), 429–441.

BIBLIOGRAPHY

Benns, Frank Lee, *The American Struggle for the British West Indies Carrying Trade, 1815–1830.* Bloomington, Indiana, 1923.
Black, Eugene C., *The Association.* Cambridge, Mass., 1963.
Board of Trade, *Report of the Lords of the Committee of Council for Trade and Plantations, on the Slave Trade to Africa and the West Indies.* London, 1789.
———, *Report of the Lords of the Committee of Council for Trade and Plantations, on Trade with America.* London, 1791.
Brooke, Richard, *Liverpool as it was during the last Quarter of the Eighteenth Century.* Liverpool, 1853.
Brougham, Henry, *An Inquiry into the Colonial Policy of the European Powers.* 4 vols., Edinburgh, 1803.
———, *An Inquiry into the State of the Nation at the Commencement of the Present Administration.* London, 1806.
———, *The Life and Times of Henry, Lord Brougham.* 3 vols., New York, 1871.
Buckingham and Chandos, Duke of, *Memoirs of the Court and Cabinets of George the Third.* 2 vols., London, 1853.
Burns, Sir Alan, *History of the British West Indies.* London, 1954.
Butterfield, Herbert, "Charles James Fox and the Whig Opposition in 1792," *Cambridge Historical Journal,* IX (1949), 292–330.
Clarkson, Thomas, *An Essay on the Slavery and Commerce of the Human Species, particularly the African.* London, 1786.
———, *An Essay on the Impolicy of the Slave Trade.* London, 1788.
Cobbett, William, *The Parliamentary History of England, from the Earliest Period to the Year 1803.* London, 1812–1820.
———, *The Parliamentary Debates from the year 1803 to the Present.* London, 1812–1820. Reprint by T. C. Hansard; corresponds to Hansard's *Debates,* first series.
Cockcroft, Grace Amelia, *The Public Life of George Chalmers.* New York, 1939.
Coupland, Reginald, "The Abolition of the Slave Trade," *Cambridge History of the British Empire,* vol. II. Cambridge, 1940.
———, *The British Anti-Slavery Movement.* London, 1964.
Currie, Dr. James, *Memoirs.* 2 vols., London, 1831.
Debrett, John, ed., *The Royal Kalendar, or Complete and Correct Annual Register.* London.
Donnan, Elizabeth, *Documents Illustrative of the History of the Slave Trade to America.* 4 vols., Washington, D. C., 1930.

Dumbell, Stanley, "The Profits of the Guinea Trade," *The Economic Journal*, II, History Supplement 1931, 254–7.
Eden, Sir Frederick Morton, *Eight Letters on the Peace, and on the Commerce and Manufactures of Great Britain and Ireland.* London, 1802.
Edinburgh Review, The.
Edwards, Bryan, *The History, Civil and Commercial of the British Colonies in the West Indies.* 2 vols., London, 1793.
Edwards, Bryan, *An Historical Survey of the Island of Saint Domingo, together with an Account of the Maroon Negroes in the Island of Jamaica, and a History of the War in the West Indies in 1793 and 1794; also, A Tour through the several islands of Barbadoes, St. Vincent, Antigua, Tobago, and Grenada, in the years 1791 and 1792, by Sir William Young.* London, 1801.
Feiling, Keith Grahame, *The Second Tory Party, 1714–1832.* London, 1938.
Foord, Archibald S., "The Waning of the Influence of the Crown," *English Historical Review*, LXII (1947).
———, *His Majesty's Opposition, 1714–1830.* Oxford, 1964.
Fraser, Lionel M., *History of Trinidad from 1781 to 1813.* 2 vols., Port of Spain, Trinidad, 1891.
Furber, Holden, *Henry Dundas, First Viscount Melville, 1742–1811.* Oxford, 1931.
Gentleman's Magazine, The.
Goebel, Dorothy Burne, "British Trade to the Spanish Colonies," *American Historical Review*, XLIII, no. 2 (January 1938), 288–321.
George, Mary Dorothy, *Catalogue of Political and Personal Satires preserved in the Department of Prints and Drawings in the British Museum.* 11 vols., London, 1942.
Granville, Castilia Countess, ed., *Lord Granville Levesen Gower: Private Correspondence, 1781–1821.* 2 vols., London, 1916.
Hall, Sir Douglas, "The West India Committee: A Historical Outline." 1956 (Typescript in the Committee's Library, London.)
Harcourt, Leveson V., *The Diaries and Correspondence of the Right Hon. George Rose.* 2 vols., London, 1860.
Harlow, Vincent T., *The Founding of the Second British Empire.* 2 vols., London, 1952.
Historical Manuscripts Commission, *Report on the Manuscripts of*

BIBLIOGRAPHY

J. B. Fortescue, Esq., preserved at Dropmore. 10 vols., London, 1892–1927.

Hochstetter Franz, "Die Wirtschaftlichen und Politischen Motive für die Abschaffung des Britischen Sklavenhandels im Jahre 1806/7," in Gustav Schmoller, ed., *Staats- und Socialwissenschaftliche Forschungen*, vol. XXV, part 1. Leipzig, 1905.

House of Commons Sessional Papers:
Note: Papers are cited by session, (order number), and volume.

1777(9)LIX	Privy Council Committee report on the African Trade, 1777.
1784(5)LXV	Privy Council Committee evidence on West India-North American trade.
1788(565)LXXX	Dimensions of slaving ships.
1789(573–6)LXXXI	Accounts of exports to Africa, to 1789.
1789(613–621)LXXXI	Imports and exports of sugar.
1789(622)LXXXII	Accounts of slaves in Jamaica.
1789(626–633)LXXXII	Accounts and papers on the slave trade.
1789(634)LXXXII	Copies of Acts for the improvement of slave conditions passed after 1786 in the West Indies.
1789(646)LXXXIV	Privy Council Committee Report on the slave trade, 1789.
1790(697–8)LXXXVII	Papers on the slave trade and minutes of evidence against abolition.
1790(699)LXXXVIII	Papers on the slave trade.
1790(705)LXXXIX	Accounts of West Indies trade.
1790–1(745–8)XXXIV	Minutes of evidence on the slave trade, taken in committee.
1791(98)XXXIX	Committee report on the slave trade.
1791(745–8)XCII	Minutes of evidence on the slave trade.
1791(766–9)XCIII	Slave trade accounts and papers.
1793(40)XL	Petition from Liverpool for commercial credit arrangements.
1793(101)XL	Report of the committee on the state of commercial credit.
1793(104)XL	Report on the financial distress in Liverpool.

1796(849)C	Accounts of slaves and imports from the West Indies.
1797–8(931)CIII	Correspondence of the Secretary of State with colonial governnors regarding Ellis's address of 1797.
1798–9(964)CVI	Accounts of ships arriving in the West Indies from Africa.
1798–9(967a)CVI	Correspondence regarding Ellis's address of 1797.
1799(964)CVI	Accounts of ships engaged in the slave trade, 1799.
1799(965)XLVIII	Papers regarding the Sierra Leone region abolition bill.
1799(965)CVII	Minutes of evidence on the Sierra Leone region abolition bill.
1799(966)CVI	Minutes of evidence on the slave trade regulating bill of 1799.
1801–2(43)IV	Accounts of loans to St. Vincent's and Grenada planters for damages suffered in Carib revolts.
1801–2(55)IV	Accounts of imports from the captured colonies.
1801–2(88)IV	Accounts of ships in the slave trade.
1803–4(72a)VII	Imports and exports of sugar.
1803–4(110)I	Abolition bill of 1804.
1803–4(119)X	Slave trade accounts and correspondence regarding Ellis's address of 1797.
1803–4(128)VIII	Slave trade accounts and papers.
1805(31)I	Abolition bill of 1805.
1805(39)X	Slave trade and abolition papers.
1805(84)IX	Slave trade shipping accounts.
1806(84)XII	Order-in-Council of 1805 and papers regarding the West Indies.
1806(91, 124)I	Bills to abolish the slave trade to foreign and captured colonies.
1806(142)XII	West Indies trade accounts.
1806(213)I	Bill to prevent new ships entering the British slave trade.
1806(265)XIII	Slave trade accounts.
1806–7(68, 92)I	Abolition bills and amendments.

1806–7(83)II	Committee report on the possible use of sugar in distilleries.
1807(65)III	Committee report on the commercial state of the West Indies.
1808(300)IV	Papers on United States-West Indian trade; 3rd report of the committee on the use of sugar in distilleries.
1826(328)XXII	Sugar prices, 1776–1826.
1831–2(381)XX	Returns on the slave population in the West Indies.
1847–8(400)LVIII	Quantities of Muscovado sugar imported into Great Britain, retained for consumption, and re-exported, 1793–1834.
1847–8(38)LVIII	Official and declared value of United Kingdom imports and exports, 1801–1846.

Howard, Robert M., ed., *Records and Letters of the Family of the Longs of Longville, Jamaica, and Hampton Lodge, Surrey.* 2 vols., London, 1925.

Hyde, Francis E., B. B. Parkinson, and Sheila Marriner, "The Nature and Profitability of the Liverpool Slave Trade," *Economic History Review*, series 2, vol. 5 (1953), no. 3.

Jarvis, Rupert C., ed., *Customs Letter-Books of the Port of Liverpool, 1711–1813.* Manchester, 1954.

Judd, Gerrit P. IV, *Members of Parliament 1734–1832.* Ames, Iowa, 1955.

King, C. R., ed., *The Life and Correspondence of Rufus King.* 6 vols., New York, 1894–1900.

Klingberg, Frank, *The Anti-Slavery Movement in England.* New Haven, 1926. Reprinted by Archon Books, 1968.

Latimer, John, *The History of the Society of Merchant Venturers of Bristol.* Bristol, 1903.

Linglebach, Anna L., "The Inception of the British Board of Trade," *American Historical Review*, XXX (July 1925).

London Gazette, The.

Long, Edward, *The History of Jamaica, or General Survey of the Antient and Modern State of that Island.* 3 vols., London, 1774.

MacInnes, C. M., *Bristol and the Slave Trade.* Bristol, 1963.

McKinnon, Daniel, *A Tour through the British West Indies, in the years 1802 and 1803, giving a particular account of the Bahama Islands.* London, 1804.

Madden, A. F. McC., "The Imperial Machinery of the Younger Pitt," in H. R. Trever-Roper, ed., *Essays in British History presented to Sir Keith Feiling.* London, 1964.

Mahan, Captain Arthur T., *The Influence of Sea Power upon the French Revolution and Empire, 1793–1812.* 2 vols., London, 1893.

Makinson, David H., *Barbados: A Study of North American-West Indian Relations, 1739–1789.* The Hague, 1964.

Malmesbury, Earl of, ed., *The Diaries and Correspondence of James Harris, First Earl Malmesbury.* 4 vols., London, 1844.

Martineau, Harriet, *An Introduction to the History of England during the Thirty Years' Peace.* London, 1851.

Matheson, Cyril, *The Life of Henry Dundas, First Viscount Melville.* London, 1933.

Mathieson, William Law, *British Slavery and its Abolition, 1823–1838.* London, 1926.

Mellor, G. R., *British Imperial Trusteeship, 1783–1850.* London, 1951.

Melville, Lewis, ed., *The Huskisson Papers.* London, 1931.

Minchinton, W. E., *The Trade of Bristol in the Eighteenth Century.* Bristol, 1957.

Mitchell, B. R., *Abstract of British Historical Statistics.* Cambridge, 1962.

Muir, John Ramsay Bryce, *A History of Liverpool.* Liverpool, 1907.

Namier, Sir Lewis B., and John Brooke, *The House of Commons, 1754–1790.* 3 vols., London, 1964.

Oliver, Vere Langford, *Caribbeana: Being Miscellaneous Papers relating to the History, Geneaology, Topology, and Antiquity of the British West Indies.* 7 vols., London, 1910–1917.

———, *The Monumental Inscriptions in the British West Indies.* Dorchester, 1927.

Pares, Richard, *A West India Fortune.* London, 1960. Reprinted by Archon Books, 1968.

———, *King George III and the Politicians.* Oxford, 1953.

———, *Merchants and Planters.* Economic History Review Supplement no. 4, Cambridge, 1960.

——, *Yankees and Creoles*. Cambridge, 1956. Reprinted by Archon Books, 1968.
Parliamentary Register, The, or History of the Proceedings and Debates in the House of Commons. London, 1774–.
Pellew, Hon. George, *The Life and Correspondence of the Rt. Hon. Henry Addington, First Viscount Sidmouth*. 3 vols., London, 1847.
Penson, Lillian M., "The London West Indian Interest in the Eighteenth Century," *English Historical Review*, XXXVIII (January 1921).
——, *The Colonial Agents of the British West Indies*. London, 1924.
Petrie, Sir Charles, *Lord Liverpool and his Times*. London, 1954.
Phillips, Ullrich B., "A Jamaica Slave Plantation," *American Historical Review*, XIX (April 1919).
Picton, J. A., *Memorials of Liverpool, Historical and Topographical*. 2 vols., Liverpool, 1907.
Ragatz, Lowell J., *Absentee Landlordism in the British West Indies*. London, 1931.
——, *A Guide to the Study of British Caribbean History, 1763–1834, Including the Abolition and Emancipation Movements*. Washington, D. C., 1932.
——, *Statistics for the Study of British Caribbean Economic History, 1763–1833*. London, 1928.
——, *The Fall of the Planter Class in the British Caribbean, 1763–1833*. New York, 1928.
Rodway, James, *History of British Guiana from 1668 to the Present*. 3 vols., Georgetown, Demerara, 1893.
Romilly, Samuel, *Memoirs of the Life of Sir Samuel Romilly, written by himself, with a selection from his correspondence*. Edited by his sons. 3 vols. in one, London, 1840.
Roscoe, Henry, *The Life of William Roscoe*. London, 1833.
Rose, John Holland, *The Life of William Pitt*. London, 1923.
Russell, Lord John, *Memorials and Correspondence of Charles James Fox*. 4 vols., London, 1853.
Sainty, J. C., *Leaders and Whips in the House of Lords, 1783–1964*. London, 1964.
Seeber, Edward D., *Anti-slavery Opinion in France during the second half of the Eighteenth Century*. London, 1937.

Sheridan, R. B., "The Commercial and Financial Organization of the British Slave Trade, 1750–1807," *Economic History Review*, XI.
Southey, Captain Thomas, *Chronological History of the West Indies*. 3 vols., London, 1827.
Stephen, James, *The Crisis of the Sugar Colonies*. London, 1802.
———, *War in Disguise, or, the Frauds of the Neutral Flags*. London, 1805.
———, *The Dangers of the Country*. London, 1807. Reprinted in part in 1807 as *New Reasons for Abolishing the Slave Trade*.
Stern, Walter M., "The London Sugar Refiners around 1800," *Guildhall Miscellany*, no. 3, February 1954.
Stockdale, J., ed., *The London Calendar, or Court and City Register*. Annual.
Sutherland, Lucy, "The City of London in Eighteenth-Century Politics," in R. Pares and A.J.P. Taylor, eds., *Essays Presented to Sir Lewis Namier*. London, 1956.
Thornton, A. P., *The Habit of Authority: Paternalism in British History*. London, 1966.
Trevelyan, George M., *Lord Grey of the Reform Bill*. London, 1929.
Tripp, Jean, "The Liverpool Movement for Abolition," *The Journal of Negro History*, XIII.
Twiss, Horace, *The Public and Private Life of Lord Chancellor Eldon*. 3 vols., London, 1844.
United States Congress, *American State Papers*, vol. VII (Class IV, Commerce and Navigation, vol. I), Washington, D. C., 1832.
United States Government, Bureau of Census, *Historical Statistics of the United States, Colonial Times to 1957*. Washington, D. C., 1960.
Vane, Charles William, Marquess of Londonderry, ed., *Correspondence, Despatches and other Papers of Viscount Castlereagh, Second Marquess of Londonderry*. 10 vols., London, 1851.
Warner, Aucher, *Sir Thomas Warner, Pioneer of the West Indies; a Chronicle of His Family*. London, 1933.
Wheatley, Henry B., ed., *The Historical and the Posthumous Memoirs of Sir Nathaniel Wm. Wraxall*. 5 vols., London, 1884.
Wilberforce, A. M., ed., *The Private Papers of William Wilberforce*. London, 1897.
Wilberforce, Robert I. and Samuel, eds., *The Correspondence of William Wilberforce*. 2 vols. in one, London, 1840.
———, *The Life of William Wilberforce*. 5 vols., London, 1838.

Williams, Eric, *Capitalism and Slavery*. Chapel Hill, North Carolina, 1944.
Williams, Gomer, *History of the Liverpool Privateers and Letters of Marque*. London, 1897.
Williams, O. C., *The Historical Development of Private Bill Procedure and Standing Orders in the House of Commons*. 2 vols., London, 1948.
Wyvill, Rev. Christopher, *Political Papers, Chiefly Respecting the ... Reformation of the Parliament of Great Britain*. York, n. d. (ca. 1800).
Young, Sir William, *The West India Commonplace Book, Compiled from Parliamentary and Official Documents; Shewing the Interest of Great Britain in the Sugar Colonies*. London, 1807.
Ziegler, Philip, *Addington: A Life of Henry Addington, First Viscount Sidmouth*. London, 1965.

Index

Abingdon, Earl of 68, 90
Abolition
 background 30–3
 bills of 1806–7, 135–8
 debates 37–49, 72–6, 80–5, 91, 93, 95–6, 99–100, 102–3, 126–8, 130, 133–4, 137–8
 of Danish slave trade 120
 of foreign slave trade 91, 93, 95, 119, 133–7, 141–3
 of slave trade to conquered colonies 105–6, 130–4, 143
Abolitionists 33, 38–42, 50–1, 53, 55, 57–60, 63, 72, 78, 96, 99, 125, 140
 and sedition 66–9, 77, 89–91, 94–5
Addington, Henry 82, 106, 125, 128–133, 136, 143
Agents, colonial 23–4
Antigua 122
Association of Friends of the People 68

Baillie, James 5n., 14

Bank of England 14n., 21–2, 116
Barbados 10, 57
Barham, Joseph Foster 99
Bastard, John 50–1
Berbice 60, 113
Board of Trade see Privy Council Committee for Trade
Bonding & Warehousing Act 116
Bosanquet, Samuel 22
Brazil 113
Brickdale, Matthew 27, 38
Bristol 25–7, 64, 72, 75, 79, 87
Burke, Edmund 73

Canning, George 56, 103, 105
Castlereagh, Lord 132, 138
Catholic Emancipation 92, 138
Chalmers, George 24, 100
Chandos, Duke of 46, 48n.
Clarence, William Duke of 84, 91, 102, 104, 129, 134n.
Clarkson, Thomas 32, 68
Compensation see Indemnities
Cuba 113

159

Currie, James 52

Demerara 60, 113
Dolben, Sir William 38–40, 48, 50
Dominica 13, 77, 111
Dundas, Henry 68, 80–5, 94, 96, 99–100, 103–4, 123, 131, 141–2

Eden, William (Lord Auckland) 36, 65, 133–4, 143
Eldon, Lord 66, 132, 138
Ellis, Charles Rose 97, 103, 123n. address of 1797, 98–100, 124, 127
Estwick, Samuel 24
Ewer, William 22, 38

Fox, Charles James 37, 50, 73, 78, 82–3, 92, 94, 100, 105, 126, 130–7, 143
Francis, Philip 78, 96
Fuller, Stephen 35, 48, 71

Gascoyne, Bamber 28, 38, 41, 73, 75
Gascoyne, Isaac 28
George III 68, 72, 89, 92, 104, 134
Gilray, cartoon 53
Glasgow 25, 87
Grenada 13, 71, 111
Grenville, W. W. 72, 77, 84–5, 90, 92, 103, 126, 133–4, 136–8, 142
Grey, Charles 131, 136
Guadaloupe 93, 110

Haiti *see* St. Domingue
Hamburg, 113–5, 118
Harris, Rev. Raymond 33
Hibbert, George 4, 22, 61
Hibbert, Robert 16
Holland, Lord 137

Indemnities 41, 45, 48–9, 65, 83, 128
Irish 128n., 129

Jamaica 58, 67, 71, 90, 93, 100, 102, 110, 114, 123, 135, 137–9, 142–3

Jay's Treaty 123
Jenkinson, Charles 25, 34–6, 42–5, 56, 60, 71–2, 74, 103–4, 106n., 123
Jenkinson, Robert Banks 82, 106n., 128, 134, 136–8, 143

Kimber, Captain 90–1
King *see* George III

Law, Edward (Ellenborough) 61, 85, 134
Leeward Island 101–2
Liverpool 3, 26, 66, 72, 74, 86, 87, 102, 116, 137
London 1, 8, 13, 18, 21–3, 109, 114
Long, Beeston 16, 21
Long, Charles 23, 79n.
Long, Edward 13, 31, 118
Long, Samuel 16, 77
Lords, House of 42, 44–9, 84–7, 90, 92, 94, 96, 100, 103, 128–9, 133–8, 142–3

Magdeburg 118
Manning, William 24, 128
Mansfield, Lord 30
Martinique 93, 113
Mathews, John 40
Middleton, Charles 39, 42, 131

Navigation laws 120–123
Neave, Richard 21
Nesbitt, John 17
Newfoundland 122
Newnham, Nathaniel 22, 74
New West India Society, Bristol 25
North American colonies 122

Orders in Council
  on U. S. trade 9, 32, 123, 134
  on conquered colonies 105–6, 130–34, 143

INDEX

Payne, Sir Ralph 59–60
Peace of Amiens 117–8, 141
Pelham, Thomas 38, 50, 106n.
Penryhn, Lord 19, 28, 38–41, 50, 73, 75, 95
Petty, Lord Henry 131–2
Piggot, Sir Arthur 133
Pinney, John 22
Pitt, William the Younger 23, 33–4, 51, 78, 89, 111–2, 119, 126, 132
 as an abolitionist 73, 92, 130
 as Parliamentary leader 36–8, 41, 45–9, 55, 65, 68, 72–3, 84, 92, 103–6, 127–9, 131, 142–3
Planters, British West Indian
 isolated from slave traders 8, 58
 economic difficulties 9–15, 32, 56, 77, 124, 126
 and navigation laws 120–4, 142
 attitudes on slaves 31, 57, 97
Portland, Duke of 92, 100, 102, 104, 142–3
Privy Council Committee for Trade 24, 34–6, 58, 70–1, 121, 124
Ramsay, James 32, 52
Regulating Act see Slave Trade Regulating Acts
Richmond, Duke of 45, 47
Rose, George 22, 79, 133
Rule of War 114

St. Domingue 65–9, 80, 90–1, 93, 110, 112–5, 117
St. Kitts 122
St. Vincent's 13, 111
Sheffield, Lord 45
Sierra Leone 78, 102
Slaves, in West Indies 10–13, 59–61
Slave Trade 1–8
 competition 5–7, 63–5, 78, 119
 deaths in 2, 38, 41, 62–3, 77
 in Africa 54–5
 suspension of 125–6
 to foreign colonies 7, 93, 119, 134

Slave Trade Regulating Acts 7, 37–58, 63–4, 66, 70–1, 94, 102, 111, 136, 142
Société des Amis des Noirs 68
Society of Merchant Venturers of Bristol 25, 72
Standing Committee see West India Planters & Merchants Society
Stanhope, Earl 42, 46
Stormont, Lord 84–5
Sugar and Sugar Trade 8–13, 109–118
Surinam 113
Sydney, Lord 45

Tarleton, Banastre 27, 69n., 76–8, 128
Tarleton, John 40, 43
Thellusson, Peter 22
Thornton, Godfrey 22
Thornton, Robert 78, 102
Thurlow, Lord 45–7, 49, 85
Tobago 93, 113
Tobin, James 25, 75n.
Trade rate 20, 72, 86–7, 135
Trinidad 60, 101, 113, 118
Tudway, Clement 17

United States 114–5, 118–9, 121–3

Watson, Brook 22, 78
West India Club, Liverpool 26
West India interest 16–17, 21
West India Merchants' Society 18–20, 72, 86, 116
West India Society of Planters and Merchants 19–20, 54, 56, 66–7, 72, 75, 77–8, 85–7, 90–1, 95–6, 105, 111–2, 120, 126, 129, 133, 135
Wilberforce, William 12, 58, 60–1, 64, 68, 73, 78–9, 81, 83, 95, 97–8, 103, 105–6, 125, 132, 136
 illness 37, 72

parliamentary leadership 53, 74–7, 79–80, 83, 90–1, 93–6, 100, 102, 106, 127–131, 140–2
animosity toward 24, 52–3, 67, 89, 133
relations with Pitt 34n., 92, 129–30
speeches and comments 67–8, 77, 80, 125–7, 132, 137–8

William, Duke of Clarence *see* Clarence
Windham, William 103

Yates, John 6
Young, Sir William 18, 24, 38, 74, 77–78, 94, 97, 99, 100, 102, 105, 130, 133